ALABAMA SHORT STORIES

VOLUME 1

SHAWN WRIGHT

SHAWN WRIGHT

Birmingham, AL 35209

shawnwright.net

Book design by Shawn Wright

ISBN: 978-1-7355822-3-8 (paperback)

ISBN: 978-1-7355822-5-2 (hardback)

This book is dedicated to my parents

Leo and Rhetta Wright

Contents

PREFACE   7

THE ICONS

Miss Liberty - Birmingham's Statue   *11*

Vulcan's Torch   *17*

USS Alabama   *23*

Miss Fancy   *31*

FIRSTS

WSY, the first radio station in Alabama   *41*

The Club at the End of the World   *49*

The First 911 Call   *55*

THE ATHLETES

Bear Bryant wants you to call your mama   *63*

Greenville Basketball   *67*

Football in the Courts: Homewood vs. Tuscaloosa   *73*

Gordie Howe Scores a Goal   *79*

ALIEN ENCOUNTERS

The Sylacauga Meteorite   *87*

Able and Baker in Space   *93*

Stars Fell on Alabama   *99*

Close Encounters in Mobile   *105*

EXCEPTIONAL PEOPLE

William Rufus DeVane King - Alabama's Vice President   *113*

The Wichahpi Commemorative Stone Wall - Tom's Wall   *119*

Fess Whatley   *125*

Ruth Elder, Pilot   *131*

Lou Wooster   *139*

THE LAND

Birmingham's Cut in Red Mountain   *149*

Where did that town name come from?   *157*

Kudzu   *169*

THE ARTISTS

She Paints on Spider Webs   *177*

The Portraits of William Frye   *185*

Clark Byers Sees Rock City   *191*

Douglas Leigh Lights Up Times Square   *197*

THE INVENTORS

Mary Anderson - Inventor of the Windshield Wiper   *207*

Andrew Jackson Beard - Inventor of the Janey Coupler   *213*

John Pratt - Inventor of the Typewriter   *219*

NOTES ON SOURCES   226
ACKNOWLEDGMENTS   253
ABOUT THE AUTHOR   255
PODCASTS   257

Preface

The 100th anniversary of Shades Cahaba School in Homewood, Alabama, was fast approaching. It was a school that my brother and I attended as well as my oldest son and his younger brother was then a student. I didn't know if the school administration was planning to celebrate this milestone, but I knew I wanted to do something. I wanted to learn more about the school, from its beginnings as a high school to an elementary school today. I talked with alumni and uncovered the truth behind stories that had been told over the years. I created the Shades Cahaba Oral History podcast and wrote the companion book soon after. Once the centennial celebration was over, I turned my attention to what was next.

I enjoyed telling stories about the school. I equally enjoyed researching, writing, and producing the podcast and book. I knew I wanted to continue writing podcasts and books, but I just needed another subject.

They say write what you know about, and I know about Alabama. I have lived here all my life, the majority in the Birmingham suburb of Homewood. And when you have been in one place as long as I have, you can't help but hear stories from around the state. Fourth grade is when you learn about civics and the state of Alabama. At least, it was for me at Shades Cahaba Elementary. *Alabama Mounds to Missiles* by Helen Morgan Akins and Virginia Pounds Brown was our textbook and was so popular with my family that my parents gave me a copy for Christmas in 1972. The book sits on my office shelf with green page markers sticking out of the top, marking story ideas.

Books such as *13 Alabama Ghosts and Jeffrey* by Kathryn Tucker Windham and elementary school field trips to Moundville, the Alabama State Capital, and the Space and Rocket Center provided me with more stories about my state. It was easy to figure out what my next podcast subject would be, Alabama.

The first episode of the Alabama Short Stories podcast was published in April 2021. That episode was about a television commercial where University of

Alabama Coach Paul "Bear" Bryant lamented that he wished he could call his mama. My father had been the creative director for this South Central Bell commercial, so I didn't have to go far for the story and give credit where credit was due. It has gone on to become the most popular episode of the series. This episode was the only interview on the podcast, but it set a tone that would continue through the following episodes.

So far, there are three seasons of ten episodes of the Alabama Short Stories podcast. True to its name, each episode is short, roughly 8 to 12 minutes each. I try to take the stories that have been told repeatedly and, through research, find a little more to the story that has not been reported.

This book is comprised of those 30 stories told in the podcast. There are stories of artists, inventors, athletes, and exceptional people from Alabama. There are icons we know and love and alien encounters. The one thing I couldn't do in the podcast was share photos. I have added pictures so you can see the people and see what they have created.

While I can't expect this book to rise to the popularity of *Mounds to Missiles* or *13 Alabama Ghosts and Jeffrey*, I hope you enjoy these stories as much as I have enjoyed sharing them with you.

Shawn Wright
Homewood, Alabama 2022

Part 1

THE ICONS

Alabama is filled with icons. Statues, buildings, signs, anything that when you see it, you know what it is, where it's located and it probably brings back memories from long ago. Maybe you visited one of these icons as a child or perhaps saw it along the interstate. It could have been a story passed down over the years that you heard so often; you could swear that you saw it yourself. Here are four stories about Alabama icons from across our state.

Miss Liberty - Birmingham's Statue

Birmingham has its share of statues around town. There are statues of people in Kelly Ingram Park, Linn Park, the UAB campus, Samford's Campus, the Birmingham Museum of Art, Five Points South, Rickwood Field, and the Alabama Sports Hall of Fame. Even Eddie Kendricks of the Temptations is on 4th Avenue North at 18th Street. I could go on and on about statues around town.

In Birmingham, the big three are Vulcan, Miss Electra, and Miss Liberty. And until 1989, they could see each other from their perches in and around downtown Birmingham.

The first statue to look over the bustling city was Miss Electra, who graces the top of the original Alabama Power Company building. Dedicated in 1926 and her original name was "Divinity of Light." Locals called her Miss Electra, which is much more fitting of a gold, nude goddess with lighting bolts in her hands and hair.

Vulcan needs no introduction. Created for the 1904 World's Fair in St. Louis, he has looked over the city from atop Red Mountain since he moved there in 1939. Finally, getting the attention, he deserved after wasting away at the Birmingham Fairgrounds.

Our subject in this story is the third statue—one who is much more chaste and serious than our first two, who are nude and partially nude. Our subject is Miss Liberty, but first, a refresher.

Our Miss Liberty is a replica of Frédéric Auguste Bartholdi's "Liberty Enlightening the World," better known as the Statue of Liberty, which has stood in New York Harbor since 1886. The statue was

Alabama Department of Archives and History.

Workers prepare to raise Miss Liberty to the top of the Liberty National Building in Birmingham's midtown.

a gift from the people of France to the United States. And to drop one more name. Gustave Eiffel built the interior metal framework. I don't think I need to tell you why he was famous.

In the 1950's Liberty National Life Insurance Company was a growing company that started as the Heralds of Liberty in Huntsville in 1900. Over the years, the company grew through acquisitions, and eventually, a holding company was created called Torchmark, now known as Globe Life Inc.

According to company history, Heralds of Liberty was somewhat of a scam and was taken over by the Alabama Insurance Department in 1921. Robert Park

Davison and Frank Park Samford took control, cleaned house, and emerged as a legitimate company called Liberty National Life Insurance Company in 1929. Just in time for the stock market crash. There is much more to this story, but let's stay on track.

By the 1950s, Frank Samford had long been the company's president, and Liberty National had continued to grow over the years. They had an impressive office in midtown in Birmingham, and what they needed was something to show off their office and their place in the insurance world.

For years the company had used the Statue of Liberty on its marketing materials and stationary. Samford decided it was time to go all in and have a statue made and placed on top of the company headquarters.

The company hired Lee and Archer Lawrie, renowned father and son sculptures, to make the plaster of paris form that the final bronze sculpture would be sculpted around.

First, however, Liberty National had to pay a fee to the Bartholdi family of $1,000 for permission to make a copy.

They could not find a forge in America that would cast a statue so large, so they went overseas. The plaster original was created in Sommervoire, Haut Marne, France and then cast by the Société Anonyme des Éstablissements Métallurgiques A. Durenne et du Val d'Osnere. The company wasn't even in the sculpting business anymore; they manufactured cast-iron pipes. But they did have history on their side. They had cast a replica of the Statue of Liberty before, which sits on the southern end of Île aux Cygnes, an artificial island built in the Seine. It is known as the Pont de Grenelle Statue of Liberty.

In a way, a pipe foundry was the perfect place to cast Birmingham's Statue of Liberty. At the time, Birmingham was the world leader in cast-iron pipe manufactured by companies such as McWane, U.S. Pipe, and American, formerly known as ACIPCO.

Our Miss Liberty is 1/5th the size of the original and was constructed in

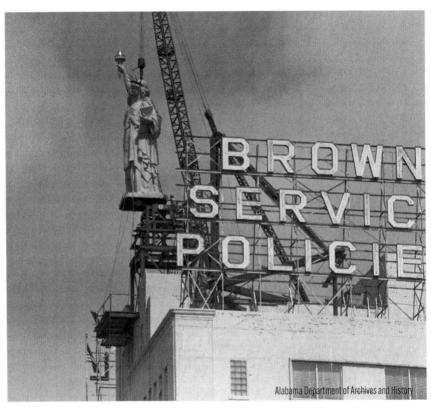

Miss Liberty raised to her perch atop the Liberty National building on 20th Street South in Birmingham.

almost the same way. It is a hollow shell with an internal steel armature inside. The bronze shell was coated with a special chemical to give it the same green patina as the original in New York harbor.

What's different about this statue is that Miss Liberty would be holding a torch with a live flame. Original plans called for electric light, but Alagasco successfully lobbied for a gas-fired flame. Engineers at Alagasco created a system with an electric self-starter in case the wind blew out the flame. The flame was lit only at night when it could be seen against the dark sky.

A pedestal was created on the top of the Liberty National building that faced west along 20th Street. A steel beam was sunk deep into the pedestal to ensure that the statue did not fall in any wind. Unfortunately, the statue is too small to venture inside like the one in New York, but there was a viewing platform on the roof of the building just below Miss Liberty so tour groups could visit and get as close as possible.

I remember going as a child and being taken to the viewing platform to see Miss Liberty. We left with plenty of Liberty National schwag such as pencils and tape measures. Honestly, I was probably as excited to get the freebies as getting close to Miss Liberty.

When Miss Liberty was completed, the casting firm was so pleased that they had a dedication ceremony before boxing her up and sending her to the port of Dunkirk to be shipped to the United States.

Shipping was a primary concern. How would they get this 31-foot tall, ten-ton statue from France to Birmingham? The first thing they had to do was remove her arm. You heard that right. They took off her arm and torch to shorten the water-tight crate she would travel in. It sounds more dramatic than it really was. It could easily be reattached in Birmingham.

At Dunkirk, Miss Liberty was loaded onto the S.S. Velma Lykes for her trip to the port of New Orleans. A crane transferred the crate to

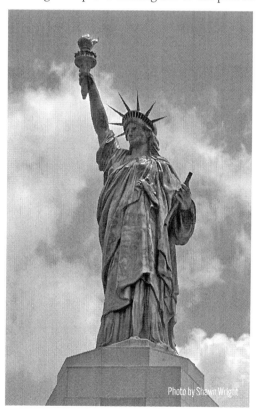

Photo by Shawn Wright

Miss Liberty today in Liberty Park. Her natural gas flame has been replaced by a gold flame similar to the original statue in New York harbor.

a rail car for the land trip north. Months before this moment, Southern Railways checked the entire 355-mile route to Birmingham to ensure that the oversized container would have sufficient clearance. One low bridge, small tunnel, or over-hanging light could spell disaster for Miss Liberty. For additional security, the train only traveled during daylight. They also did it on Sunday when there would be less traffic.

After an uneventful trip to Birmingham, Miss Liberty made the short trip from the rails to the Liberty National Office. She was uncrated, her arm reat-tached, stood upright, and then draped in cloth for the unveiling.

There was a ceremony with music and speeches. Sculptor Archer Lawrie was there, and Frank Samford III unveiled Miss Liberty. Then the crowd watched her take the final part of the journey, 175-feet straight up.

It wouldn't be the last time she moved.

In the 1970s, Liberty National created Torchmark Corporation as a holding company and acquired Globe Life and Accident. By the 1980s, Torchmark entered the real estate development field and created Liberty Park along with Drummond Company. A residential, office, retail, and golf development that would soon be annexed into Vestavia Hills. Miss Liberty made her final move from midtown to a new tower at the entrance to Liberty Park.

You can visit Miss Liberty today. She is adjacent to the Greater Alabama Council, Boy Scouts of America office. If you are traveling on I-459 South of Birmingham, she is prominently featured at a bend in the interstate.

Some miss seeing her in midtown, but her new home in the suburbs is more her style. She is probably happy to leave the big city behind for those more risque statues.

Vulcan's Torch

There are many statues located in and around Birmingham. The big three include Miss Liberty, Miss Electra and the king, or god of them all, Vulcan. In this story, we are going to talk about Vulcan's torch. But first, a little history lesson for those not familiar with Vulcan and why he is on Red Mountain.

Iron built Birmingham. Not just the buildings but the economy. It takes three raw materials to make steel; limestone, iron ore, and coal. All three are found in abundance around Birmingham. Birmingham was founded in 1871, and the city exploded in growth. So much so that it was called the Magic City. By the end of the 19th century, Birmingham was the third-largest exporter of pig iron globally, producing 3/4 of the United States' exports.

This upstart city was ready to flex its muscles and show the rest of the country what was happening in Birmingham. The 1904 Louisiana Purchase Exhibition in St Louis, Missouri, was chosen as the venue. The exhibition was also known as the 1904 World's Fair. Birmingham planned to contribute the raw materials from the area when they learned that Alabama would not have an official exhibit. The Commercial Club of Birmingham decided to submit its plan to highlight Birmingham. Instead of sending the raw materials, what if they created a "giant man" made of those materials. I am sure there were many suggestions about what this "giant

Courtesy of Library of Congress

Vulcan on display in the Mines Building at the World's Fair, St. Louis, Missouri.

man" would look like, but somewhere along the way, they settled on Vulcan, the Roman god of fire which included the fire of volcanoes, deserts, metalworking, and the forge.

The committee set out to find their sculptor, and Giuseppe Moretti was commissioned.

When Vulcan was depicted in sculpture and art through the centuries, he was usually shown with a blacksmith's hammer, and Moretti followed tradition. His Vulcan would have a raised arm with a spear in his hand. Vulcan looked down the shaft to make sure his spear was straight and true.

Vulcan wore what I suppose would be a leather apron and nothing else. His backside was exposed to the world. How that got past any committee in the early 20th century in Alabama is beyond me. Can you imagine the uproar today if that was proposed?

Once Moretti's clay model was approved, he set about production on what would become the largest cast-iron statue in the world. His team created a full-size version of Vulcan in plaster at his studio in Passaic, New Jersey. The statue was made in sections so that it could be taken apart and shipped by train to Birmingham and the former Hood Foundry. The foundry was located at First Avenue North and 14th Street. Workers would use each section of plaster to create the molds that the iron would be poured into, making the final pieces.

The statue was completed on time and sent to St. Louis. It made a huge impression on visitors. It was displayed in the Palace of Mines and Metallurgy, winning the "grand prize." The statue was so popular that the cities of St. Louis, San Fransisco, and Portland wanted the statue for their towns. There was even a proposal for the statue to be in the middle of the Chesapeake Bay.

In 1905 the statue made its way back to Birmingham and was deposited by the side of the rail tracks due to unpaid freight bills. The trip back damaged Vulcan's arm, and his spear point was lost, which is where our story is going.

But what to do with Vulcan? Proposals ranged from having him in the middle of what we now know as Linn Park to the center of the Five Points Circle. Vulcan's bare bottom was probably too much for the residents to have looming above them, so both ideas were dismissed.

Vulcan was moved to the Alabama State Fairgrounds, where he could be displayed until a more permanent place was found. He was incorrectly reassembled, with his arm twisted, the hammer and anvil behind him, and no spear in his hand. Without the spear, the State Fair authorities could use his hand for advertising purposes. He advertised Sherwin-Williams paints, Heinz pickles, and Coca-Cola, among others.

After 30 years of being an advertising shill at the fairgrounds, an appropriate home was found for Vulcan. The Tennessee Coal, Iron and Railroad Company (TCI) donated five acres of former mining land above Lone Pine Gap. Local groups raised funds, and with help from the Works Progress Administration, they came together to fund and complete a 124-foot tall pedestal where Vulcan would be placed. A new, smaller spear was created and added to Vulcan's hand.

Thirty-five years after he was created and sent to St. Louis, Vulcan finally had a home high above the city it was designed to celebrate.

The new spear created for Vulcan at this new home would not stay visible for long.

For all of us who were alive at the end of the 20th century, we didn't know about Vulcan's spear. We only knew about the light he held in his hand. A green or red popsicle that he was offering to the gods in his raised hand. This neon torch was all we knew, but why was it there?

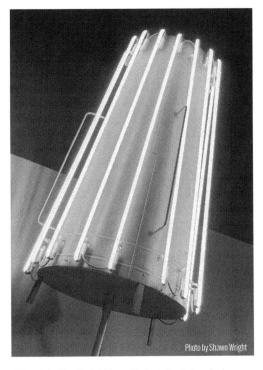

Photo by Shawn Wright

The original traffic light is on display in the Vulcan Park museum.

The Birmingham Junior Chamber of Commerce, better known as the Jaycees, was organized in 1920 to provide young adults with networking opportunities and learn business skills. Leadership training was achieved through the roles taken on in projects they ran.

In 1946, R. Paul Moon, chairman of the Jaycees' safety committee, was looking for a project to help reduce the increasing amount of deaths on the roads around Birmingham. He got the idea that a color-coded safety beacon that signaled when someone died in a car wreck would remind others to be careful on our roads. Moon's original idea was to have a beacon placed atop the flagpole outside the West End Library. Another idea was to put it on top of the Comer Building, what we know as the City Federal Building, which would be much more visible. Then someone came up with having Vulcan be the bearer of bad news.

A proposal was submitted to the Birmingham Parks and Recreation Board for a temporary torch wrapped around the existing spear. The proposal was accepted, and the Jaycees' campaign to fund the project went into high gear. The cone was designed to spin so that Alabama Neon Sign Company workers could easily replace each of the sixteen neon tubes.

If adding light to Vulcan's spear wasn't bad enough, metal climbing rungs were welded to his left hip and up across his chest to the arm. Cables were attached to his right hand and were strung to Vulcan's shoulder to help the worker climb the arm to the light. Work was completed, and a light switch was installed in the guard's room at the tower's base.

For the next 53 years, the torch glowed green. When there was a traffic fatality, the light was changed to red. The idea was that motorists who saw the red light would be reminded to drive safely and watch out for others.

From the front porch of my house in Homewood, I could see whether the torch was green or red. I don't know if the campaign saved lives, but I do know that it made a big impression on me. A red light was something that we did not want to see.

Photo by Shawn Wright

Vulcan as he looks today with the restored spear in his right hand.

By the end of the 20th century, Vulcan had spent half its life on that pedestal above the city, and it was falling apart. Updates needed to be made, and Vulcan was dismantled and sent to Robinson Iron in Alexander City for refurbishment. They also made a new spear for Vulcan to hold. The torch was being replaced. But not without controversy. Some people don't like change, and former mayor George Seibels probably spoke for most of them when he said, "it would be a total disaster to even consider taking the torch down."

While Vulcan was in rehab, the entire Vulcan Park site was updated or, in some cases going back to the way things were. The updates in the 1970s were removed, a new elevator was installed, a museum was created, and other updates were made. When Vulcan returned, his position was adjusted slightly to the east for a better profile view and Vulcan's anvil and hammer placement. It also meant that Homewood no longer received the full view of Vulcan's derriere. Homewoods view of Vulcan's backside was popularized in 1982 by the song "Moon Over Homewood," written by WYDE-AM disc jockey Jack Voorhies.

If you never saw the torch in Vulcan's hand, you are still in luck; you can see it to this day in the museum at Vulcan Park.

Courtesy of Library of Congress

Vulcan on display in the Mines Building at the World's Fair, St. Louis, Missouri.

USS Alabama

Cities around Alabama all seem to have an icon that identifies them. Huntsville has the Saturn Rocket, Birmingham has Vulcan, Montgomery has the capital, and Tuscaloosa and Auburn have stadiums dwarfing their cities. Mobile has an icon as well, the World War II battleship USS Alabama.

The USS Alabama in Mobile bay is one of those must-visit attractions around the state. And if you have been in Cub Scouts, Boy Scouts, or Girl Scouts, there is a good chance you have spent at least one night on the ship the way thousands of service members did on active duty.

I have spent three or four nights on the USS Alabama when I took both of my sons on cub scout trips. Every time we went, we stayed at the bow of the ship. We followed our guides through a large hatch and down steep stairs. We walked around a large curved wall that was part of the forward gun to the very front

★ MOBILE

of the bow. There would be bunks two and three high that we would sleep in overnight. You could see the bow curve on the walls, and there were cylinders that cut through the room, housing the large chains connecting to the anchors. We had adequate bathroom facilities, air conditioning, and mattresses that rested on cots with springs. If not for the snoring of the other adults, it would have been very comfortable. It was a lot like what the sailors went through during wartime, except they did not have air conditioning, and the bunk rooms would get very hot.

I had inside knowledge of what life was like aboard an active battleship. My grandfather, Marion Ramsey McQueen, was a career navy man, rising to the rank of Chief Petty Officer. He joined in the 1920s and happened to be on the USS Maryland when the Japanese attacked Pearl Harbor. Luckily he survived and was able to tell me a little about life aboard a battleship.

There were a lot of sailors on a battleship, and they slept in every available space. My grandfather told me that he slept in a hammock. There would be hooks hanging from poles to hang your hammock. When you walk around the USS

Alabama, you will notice poles with hooks on them all over the ship. It looks a little like you could be in a meat locker and almost see sides of beef hanging on the hooks.

I believe these hooks are where some sailors hung their hammocks to sleep at night. The hammocks were one size fits all, and I never asked granddad how he could get his 6'2" frame onto the small hammocks.

The attack on Pearl Harbor decimated the U.S. Pacific fleet. The battleships were in port, and lucky for us, our aircraft carriers were at sea during the attack. The battleships USS Arizona (BB-39) and USS Oklahoma (BB-37) were sunk in the initial attack and lost. The USS Nevada (BB-36) was refloated and repaired. The USS California (BB-44) and the USS West Virginia (BB-48) sustained damage and sunk into the mud. They were refloated, repaired, and put back into service.

My grandfather's ship, the USS Maryland, was lucky enough to be docked between the USS Oklahoma and Ford Island, protecting them from the worst that the USS Oklahoma had gone through. The USS Maryland was sent to Puget Sound for repairs and modernization before joining the remaining fleet at the Battle of Midway.

Many of these ships had been launched 20 years before the attack on Pearl Harbor. Luckily, the newest battleships, the South Dakota Class, were being constructed at Navy Yards around the U.S., including BB-60, The USS Alabama.

When she entered service, she was deployed to strengthen the British Home Fleet and protected convoys to the Soviet Union. She transferred to the Pacific in 1943 and was part of the Gilbert and Marshall Islands campaign. She was an escort for a carrier task force and took part in the Mariana and Palau Islands campaigns and the Philippines campaign. In 1945, she received a retrofit and made it back for the Battle of Okinawa and attacks on the Japanese mainland. After the Japanese surrendered, she participated in Operation Magic Carpet, bringing over 700 men home from the former war zone.

After the war, the USS Alabama was assigned to the Pacific Reserve Fleet until

USS Alabama (BB-60) is towed into Puget Sound on the start of her last voyage to Mobile, Alabama in 1964

1962, when she was stricken from the Naval Vessel Register. This was the end of the road for the once-proud USS Alabama. Or was it?

Jimmy Morris was having breakfast and reading the May 1, 1962 edition of the Mobile Register newspaper when a story caught his eye. The Associated Press was reporting that the South Dakota class of battleships would be sold for scrap, including the USS Alabama.

When Morris made it to work at the Tourist & Visitors Department of the Mobile Area Chamber of Commerce, he found Stephen Croom, chairman of the Chamber's Committee for Preservation of Historic Landmarks, already eager to join the fight to save the USS Alabama.

They built a team of businessmen who agreed that the battleship should be preserved as a memorial to Alabama citizens who fought here and abroad in World War II. They met with Governor John Patterson, who was in complete agreement. A petition was immediately sent to the Alabama State Legislature, and a joint resolution was passed.

The Governor put together a fact-finding committee to study the feasibility of bringing the ship to the port of Mobile. This was not the first battleship to be saved from the scrapyard. The USS North Carolina (BB-55) and USS Texas (BB-35) had been saved and relocated to their home states. Both groups were eager to share their expertise to help save the USS Alabama.

While the committee worked, a statewide election was held, and George Wallace became Alabama's newest Governor. Luckily he fully supported the actions of committee members and helped to "bring the Alabama home."

The State of Alabama was fully behind the effort, and surprisingly, so was the national government. The only problem was, where was the money going to come from?

The Navy was going to give the USS Alabama to the state. The transfer was "as is, where is," with no additional cost to the Federal Government. "As is" meant the state was getting the ship in the shape it was currently in. And after being mothballed for the past 15 years, it needed some work. "Where is" meant the state had to move it from the Pacific Reserve Fleet in Puget Sound, outside of Bremerton, Washington, all the way to Mobile Bay.

The Navy would be allowed to inspect the USS Alabama annually and make sure she was in fighting shape. A provision was made that should the Navy ever need her; they reserved the right to send her back into active duty status. A lot of work would have to be done to get her into shape. Scraping and repainting every inch of the ship was job one.

Moving the USS Alabama would be no easy task. It was a long journey from Puget Sound to Mobile Bay, and the state would have to pay to get the ship home.

With all the help the state government was giving the newly formed Battleship Commission, none was financial. Public fundraising was the only answer.

Frank Samford, Chairman of Birmingham-based Liberty National Life Insurance Company, rallied the state's life insurance agents and underwriters. While collecting monthly policy premiums, they asked citizens for donations in a statewide grassroots fundraising campaign.

The most impressive part of the fundraising campaign was the Children's

USS Alabama (BB 60) moves through Gaillard (Culebra) Cut in the Panama Canal

Campaign. Children of Alabama donated almost $100,000 in nickels, dimes, and quarters to save the Alabama. In exchange, Governor Wallace promised those who donated, one free ticket to visit the USS Alabama as long as he was in office.

A professional fundraising company was hired to help raise money from corporations and make up the difference. In less than six months, $800,000 was raised in all efforts, enough to get the ship moving to Alabama. The Navy executed a transfer document to the State of Alabama, and the battleship set sail.

The trip from Puget Sound to Mobile Bay would be 5,600 miles long and travel through the Panama Canal. Two tugs, the Sea Ranger and the Sea Lion would be tasked with towing the battleship to Alabama. What would seem to be a simple task had its challenges.

As the USS Alabama approached Panama around Cape Mala, The tug Sea Lion lost its ability to steer and got tangled up in the heavy tow chain. She rolled over and sank with one crewman lost.

One tugboat was not enough to safely haul the USS Alabama through the Panama Canal and then to Mobile. The tug Margaret Walsh joined Sea Ranger about a week later to continue the trip.

On August 26, 1964, Panama Canal Senior Pilot Captain Irving Hay boarded the Alabama to guide her through the canal, a great honor for him. The Governor of the Panama Canal Zone had a request. He wanted them to go through the east side locks so that spectators could more easily view the ship. Thousands gathered at each of the locks.

After the tragedy in the Pacific, the trip through the locks was uneventful. But a tropical storm approaching the Gulf of Mexico would delay them even more. The gulf had become churned up due to Tropical Storm Dora, slowing the tugs as they moved towards Mobile. The storm did a lot of damage in Florida, but luckily it turned back towards the Atlantic, leaving Mobile alone to welcome the USS Alabama.

After 56 days, on September 14, 1964, the USS Alabama entered Mobile Bay and stopped close to her final destination. She was moored just offshore as she waited for dredging to be completed so she could be towed into her final destination.

Alabama Department of Archives and History.

USS Alabama (BB-60) is welcomed into Mobile Bay on September 14, 1964

A hand-picked crew of mainly navy veterans began work seven days a week, stripping, priming, and painting the old gray lady. The interior of the ship had to be cleaned and made accessible for the general public to tour. Four months later, the ship was ready for its first visitors.

Two thousand spectators watched as Governor Wallace officially opened the USS Alabama Battleship Memorial Park on January 9, 1965. Eighteen years to the day that the Alabama had been put into mothballs.

Battleship Memorial Park has been a top tourist attraction in Alabama for over 50 years. The park is much different today than it was in 1964. Today you can visit the USS Drum Submarine and an impressive number of military planes.

During her career as a museum ship, Alabama has been used as a set for several movies, including "Under Siege" in 1992, starring Steven Seagal, Tommy Lee Jones, and Gary Busey. And the "USS Indianapolis: Men of Courage" in 2016 starring Nicolas Cage.

If you haven't visited the USS Alabama, you need to check that off your list. And if you ever get the chance to spend the night on the USS Alabama, do so. Just one suggestion. Make sure you take some earplugs.

Miss Fancy

The Avondale community of Birmingham has been going through a renaissance in the past decade. For years the community seemed like an afterthought, a neighborhood you drove through to get to work or some other place. Citizens had been moving into homes and renovating them for some time, and artists already had studios in the area. But a little over a decade ago, business owners decided to take a chance on Avondale. They have opened up music venues, restaurants, and even a couple of breweries. The renaissance had started.

"Big Spring" was well known to stagecoach drivers in the mid 19th century. Located near the junction of Georgia Road and Huntsville Road, it was proclaimed to have the sweetest waters in the region. The spring surfaced from a cavern that became accessible in the mid-1880s. Explorers at the time reported finding arrowheads and carved out niches, proof of ancient residents. A 20-foot deep crystal clear channel was

BIRMINGHAM

Alabama Department of Archives and History.

Miss Fancy on her morning walk in the Avondale Zoo with keeper, Dayton Allen.

described as well. Stories were told about this channel as part of a more extensive river system underneath the city of Birmingham. Early settlers were told stories by local Indians who spoke of an underground river that ran the valley's length. This legend seemed to grow with every telling.

The springs had been diverted into channels in the appropriately named Spring Street that started at the park's gates. As the city around Avondale grew, the springs were directed to the stormwater drains running underneath Spring Street, what is now known as 41st Street.

Peyton King owned the land around the spring, and he sold it to the Avondale Land Company. Along with surrounding land, they incorporated the area as the city of Avondale, named after a Cincinnati, Ohio, suburb which had been named for the Avondale Parish in Scotland. As a condition of selling the land, King specified that the spring and the 40 acres around it would remain a public park. The area around the springs had been a popular picnic spot for early Birmingham residents for years.

King's house was on the North West corner of what would become Avondale park. It was torn down and replaced with a Carnegie Library, one of the few in the Birmingham area. In 1961, the Carnegie Library was demolished and replaced with the current library building.

The city would triple in size in the next decade, and Avondale was eventually annexed into the rapidly expanding Birmingham City limits. The area's primary industry was a textile mill founded in 1897 by future Governor B.B. Comer. It took its name from the fledgling city and was known as Avondale Mills for the next century until its closing in 2006.

Avondale Park was, for years, the largest park in Birmingham. There were ballfields and a pavilion, and the Big Spring would fill a wading pool. The park was at the base of a steep hill, and a Villa was constructed on top. On the slope between the pond and the villa, the Works Project Administration created an outdoor amphitheater.

But what was most unique about the park in its early days was not all these attractions but a small zoo.

The first zoo in Birmingham was just a small collection of exotic animals located in the Birmingham Fire Station No. 3 located at Magnolia Park and 22nd Street. They moved it into Magnolia park as the collection grew, now known as Brother Bryan Park. In 1911, the animals from Magnolia Park and a group of animals at East Lake Park were all relocated to a new exhibit in Avondale Park.

Over the years, the Avondale Zoo would house various animals, including a bison, two cows, a llama, two black bears, foxes, wolves, coyotes, raccoons, and wildcats. There were monkeys, rabbits, swans, waterfowl, alligators, peacocks, hawks, owls, goats, and a supposedly 8-foot long eastern diamondback rattlesnake named Dick. Area residents supplied the zoo with some of these animals. They were probably pets that had become unwieldy to handle. For instance, explorer Donald Beaty brought home a jaguar cub from his travels to the Amazon. Once the cub started to grow, he decided a zoo would be a better place to keep a wild animal.

There were a wide variety of animals in the zoo, but from the beginning, officials had their eye on a larger marquee animal.

The Hagenbeck-Wallace Circus was a huge circus that toured the United States. At the time, it was the second-largest circus next to Ringling Brothers and Barnum and Bailey. When they visited Birmingham in 1912, zoo officials inquired about purchasing an Asian elephant. Money was raised through civic promotions, and a kids' penny drive raised $500 towards the purchase.

In November 1913, the zoo was ready. Birmingham Age-Herald Editor E. W. Barrett, Birmingham Park Director Frank Smith, and Park Commissioner, James Wilson, took the train to meet the circus in Tuscaloosa. Because where else in Alabama should you buy an elephant?

After watching the show, Mr. Barrett chose a female elephant named "Fanchon." Someone in Missouri, not the circus, owned Fanchon, so long-distance negotiations took place, and a $2,000 price was agreed upon. The money was wired to the owner, and the elephant was headed to Birmingham.

I thought it was curious that a third party owned the elephant and not the circus. But in March of that year, while the circus was at their winter headquarters in Peru, Indiana, the great flood of 1913 occurred. The circus tragically lost eight elephants, 21 lions and tigers, and eight performing horses in the floodwaters. Rival circuses came to their rescue and loaned them animals and equipment so they could get back on the road in April.

Fanchon was taken to the train station, and after some deft maneuvering, she was loaded onto an L&N railway baggage car, breaking a light or two along the way. Circus handler, Curly Hayes, made the trip as well. He would make sure that Fan-

Two women from Macon, Georgia visiting Miss Fancy at the Avondale Zoo

chon made it to Birmingham and that her new handler was well trained for the job.

While the name Fanchon might have been great in the circus, it doesn't roll off the tongue. And it's not the name you want your star attraction to be known. By the time she was delivered to Birmingham, they had changed her name to "Miss Fancy."

Miss Fancy's arrival in the city was quicker than expected, and a proper house for her was not yet completed at the zoo. She spent the first night at the Gipsy Smith Auditorium, located on 1st Avenue between 22nd and 23rd street. The Birmingham Ad Club was holding a Home Products Show, and Miss Fancy would make her debut to the community there. She would spend the night in the auditorium on mattresses donated by Perfection Mattress Company of Birmingham. An original sponsor of the event.

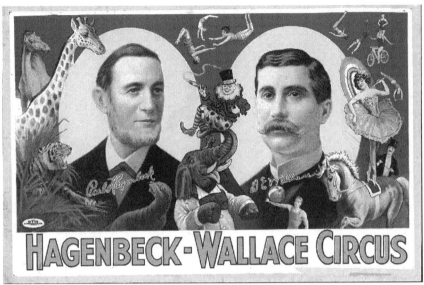

The next day, Miss Fancy would visit the zoo. But first, she would call on the Age-Herald building and Editor E.W. Barrett before making her way south along Twentieth Street to Five Points South. Miss Fancy would walk past the stately mansions on Highland Avenue, past Lakeview Park, and then on to Avondale Park. She would spend the day there before returning to the auditorium.

Miss Fancy had one more home before her permanent home at the zoo was completed. The Home Products Show had ended, and the auditorium would be torn down. She received an invitation from the Peerless Lumber Company, where she could stay in a heated building until she moved permanently to the zoo.

The great thing about Miss Fancy was she was a trained circus performer. She was used to large crowds and screaming children. When she got to Birmingham, she was not fazed by the attention and the masses. Many pictures of Miss Fancy show this. There are photos of children at her feet or climbing on top of her as she lay on the ground. The kids loved it, and it seems Miss Fancy also loved the attention.

John Todd would become her new trainer after Curly Hayes rejoined the circus. At the time, he was the only African-American elephant handler in the United States. Todd was responsible for feeding her and mucking out her pen. He would trim her toenails and tusks and give her plenty of exercise. They would often take 5-10 mile walks through the surrounding neighborhood. The two would become very close.

Miss Fancy weighed 1,800 lbs. when she first came to the Avondale Zoo. When Todd left for a year's service in the Army during World War 1, it greatly affected Miss Fancy. She was sad and wouldn't eat. By the time Todd returned, Miss Fancy only weighed 1,100 lbs. Once her appetite returned, a typical daily feeding for Miss Fancy included 175 lbs. of hay, 45 gallons of oats, and 110 gallons of water.

As you can imagine, the fencing used to keep Miss Fancy in her pen is not the same as what is used at the Birmingham Zoo today. From time to time, Miss Fancy would tire of her pen and break out and explore the neighborhood. In one incident, she wandered off from the park and took a stroll on Overlook Road, on the hill above the park. Frightened parents gathered curious children into homes and called the police. They found Miss Fancy grazing on shrubs and small trees in the yards of the neighborhood homes. All it took was for her caretaker, John Todd, to point her in the direction of the park, and they headed off together.

There had been other stories of people opening the curtains of their homes, only to see an elephant looking back at them through the window. I imagine it was exciting and terrifying all at the same time.

When I had a dog would never take his medicine. I always had to hide it in something he loved, like peanut butter. Miss Fancy was no different. When she needed to take medication, the only way she would take it was to mix it with whiskey. Keep in mind that from 1920 on, prohibition was the law of the land. At the recommendation of a veterinarian, the city commission would donate whisky confiscated by county prohibition agents. A quart or more of whisky would be required for each dose.

All that whisky would have been hard to ignore during the depths of prohibition, and we know that John Todd was human. From time to time, he would share the whisky with Miss Fancy. We know this because Todd was arrested at least once for drunkenness. No word if they were able to arrest Miss Fancy as well.

By the 1930s, the depression had its grip on Birmingham and the nation. It was no longer feasible to fund and maintain a zoo, especially when one of your animals eats as much as Miss Fancy did.

She was sold to the Cole Brothers-Clyde Beatty Circus and renamed "Frieda." She is mentioned in the circus handbook from 1934 as the circus prepared for the winter circuit. "New animals were arriving including "Freida," a giant elephant from Birmingham, Alabama, who towered over the other three in the elephant row. Freida tips the scales at 8,600 pounds."

It would be another two decades before the people of Birmingham would see elephants outside of the circus. They would not have a zoo until the Birmingham Zoo, located on the other side of Red Mountain in Shades Valley, opened in 1955.

Miss Fancy might have left Avondale in 1934, but her legend continues. She was referenced in a couple of books, notably Fannie Flagg's "Fried Green Tomatoes at the Whistle Stop Cafe." She is also remembered fondly in the resurgent Avondale Community. A statue of Miss Fancy is located at Avondale Park. There was a restaurant called "Fancy's on Fifth" and the Avondale Brewing Company, which was one of the first businesses to move back into the community, uses Miss Fancy as an icon.

So what became of Miss Fancy? According to one source, she died 20 years later in 1954 in Buffalo, New York. If that is correct, she would have been in her 80s which is very old for an elephant.

Part 2

FIRSTS

It seems that everyone wants to be first.

They want to be in first place in a race,

the first person to accomplish a feat,

the first person to invent a product,

or maybe the first to climb a mountain.

For some people, it's just for fun.

But for others, it can be all-consuming

and possibly life-threatening obsession.

Here are three stories about firsts in Alabama.

WSY, the first radio station in Alabama

Not only do we get radio from towers located around the state, but we can also now get it from satellites. We can also get a form of radio as podcasts which you download to your phone or electronic device to listen to at your leisure. Some may argue that podcasts are not radio at all, but we can all agree that radio has been around all our lives. In Alabama, it started almost 100 years ago.

There were very few companies in the early 1920s that had any experience with the high-powered electricity it took to build and run a radio station. If it was going to get done, Alabama Power was going to have to do it.

The original purpose of an Alabama Power radio station was not to provide entertainment to the citizens of Alabama. It was intended to keep in touch with line crews in isolated areas around the state. To send them information, weather forecasts, whatever they needed.

One of the first visitors to the new studio was

The WSY Studio. The microphone is the arched piece of furniture directly behind the pianist.

Alabama Power President Thomas Martin. He gave a short four-minute talk and then, with tongue firmly planted in cheek, spoke to the "thousands of listeners." Martin was a big supporter of the radio station. If the name Martin rings a bell, Lake Martin and Martin dam are named in his honor.

It took a while for the studio to be constructed, and they would do test broadcasts every day while they dialed in the settings. They would broadcast something like:

"Hello Jones, hello Gadsden, Mary, Mary, quite contrary, 1, 2, 3, 4. How do you like the sound, etc. etc."

Soon after, letters started coming in faster and faster from locations outside of Alabama, such as Florida, New York, Michigan, Kansas, and Oklahoma.

The publicity department saw a new opportunity and got busy, working out the programs and booking bands for a full-fledged radio station. If you've got the equipment and the public is interested in this new technology, why not broadcast some entertainment for their pleasure.

Back before the airwaves were littered with thousands of radio and television stations, wifi and cell service. A broadcasting station could be heard for miles, thousands of miles even. WSY managers believed their signal could be heard for 500 miles, but if the atmosphere cooperated, it could go three or four times that far.

There were only about 250 radio stations in 1922, and the programs could be picked up almost anywhere. Receiving the programs was great for people who lived out in the country. People who were too far to get same-day newspaper delivery could be up to date on current events. And even those without electricity could benefit. Most radios at that time were built from kits and ran on batteries.

The WSY studio was located at 1921 Powell Avenue by the Powell Steam Plant. There were two rooms. One had the broadcast equipment, and the other was a studio or "concert room" with a sofa, piano, Victrola, and a "radiophone," a large microphone mounted on a wooden stand.

During the testing, Dr. Courtney Shropshire chartered the Vicksburg chapter of the Civitan Club, a volunteer club that Dr. Shropshire had started in Birmingham in 1917. Over 500 letters were received from all over the country. Several letters came from California and one from the S.S. Tuscania, who heard the presentation far off Cape Charles, Virginia, in the Atlantic. It did not say so in the article, but you have to believe that this broadcast helped the growth of the Civitan during this time.

The first WSY broadcast was on April 24, 1922, only two years after the first broadcasts happened in the U.S. and England. The broadcast day probably started at 5 a.m. so that early rising farmers would get the day's information. The announcer signed on:

"This is WSY, the radio phone broadcasting station of the Alabama Power Company, located at Birmingham, Alabama. To enable you to tune your instruments, we will now play a phonograph record selection."

The announcer would then put a record on the Victrola, and the radiophone

Courtesy of Alabama Power Company Corporate Archives

The WSY control room

would pick up the music and broadcast it. Each day's broadcast would also include featured news, market and farm reports, closing stock quotations, and a Bible discussion or an organ recital from one of the five churches that were hard-wired to the station.

There was also what you might call a talk show in the afternoon or early evening. It might be a well-known person or celebrity passing through the state, or maybe there was talk of what was happening at Alabama Power or an industrial topic.

Music clubs from around the state were invited to play in the evening hours. The show would be broadcast three days a week with mainly the WSY Orchestra playing. The orchestra was made up of Alabama Power employees.

All the players had to get used to the studio. Most were comfortable playing on a stage in front of a crowd. Now had to play in the cramped confines of the WSY studio.

One evening a jazz band was featured, and they asked the listening audience what they would like to hear for an encore. Within minutes the radio operator was inundated with requests from as far away as Michigan and Southern Louisiana. They had to tell the audience to stop calling in as the switchboard was swamped.

The studio was quickly replaced with an updated studio on the top floor of the four-story Loveman, Joseph & Loeb's department store on third avenue north. It's where the McWane Center is now. Acoustics experts said it was the finest in the world. At least that was what the Birmingham News wrote. The station had a display window on the street level with a large map of the United States. On the display floor were letters from enthusiastic listeners, and string connected the letters to the location they came from on the map.

In the fall of 1922, WSY made plans to broadcast the southern championship football game between Auburn and Georgia Tech being held in Atlanta.

A special wire was run from Atlanta to Bernheim Electric Company in Birmingham and Neal Electric Company in Bessemer to receive constant updates. WSY had an announcer that understood the game of football and could take the terse telegraphic communications and recreate the game for the listener to hear. As the paper said, "it will make the listener almost believe that he is following the ball with his own eyes."

A month after the new studio was opened, a February ice storm shut Birmingham off from the rest of the world. Telephone and telegraph lines were down. All the newspaper presses were shut down, which is just as well since they couldn't get the AP and UPI wire services reports.

WSY became the lifeline to the outside world by broadcasting news about what was happening in Birmingham. And they reported what was happening in the outside world to Birmingham citizens. The station even helped with personal issues. One woman got to her brother in Pittsburgh to make sure he got to their dying father's bedside, and they reached out to a visitor in Cleveland to let him know that his son died suddenly in Birmingham.

Alabama Power Company Corporate Archives.

Band in the WSY Studio.

The storm also allowed Alabama Power the opportunity to go back to the station's original mission. They were able to broadcast load dispatching to Anniston, Gadsden, and Warrior to coordinate the movement of lineman and construction crews to Birmingham.

To help brand the station, WSY created a trademark featuring a Vulcan-type figure. Even though Birminghams Vulcan had been cast in 1904 for the St. Louis World's fair, the statue may have been at the Birmingham Fairgrounds and not looking over the city as the icon it is now. The WSY Vulcan was a Norse-looking figure with a winged helmet striking an anvil with a hammer and bolts of electricity shooting up. And this Vulcan seems to be wearing a complete set of clothes. The slogan was "Service from the Heart of Dixie." Alabama's state nickname.

An employee came up with the design in a contest and won $25 from Alabama Power President Martin. That is roughly $385 today.

At the end of the broadcast day, the sign off would be:

"The anvil symbolizes the city of Birmingham, iron, and steel working center of the south, and home of WSY. One stroke of the anvil stands for health, one for happiness and the third for prosperity. All three Alabama gives in unlimited measure."

Three slow strikes of the anvil followed. The announcer bade the audience good night as the last one faded away.

And it's hard to believe, but there was no advertising on WSY. The entire effort was undertaken as a public service. Alabama Power even invited every state chamber of commerce to promote their communities on the air.

The station's popularity was also the reason the company decided to shutter the station in late 1923. The publicity department was dedicating too much time to running the station and not enough time to the company's business. When they realized that it was time to hire full-time talent for the station, that was when they knew it was time to get out of the radio business.

President Martin felt that the companies mission to pioneer radio broadcasting in the south had been accomplished. The station stopped broadcasting on November 6, 1923, not even two years after the station signed on.

Over 10,000 letters had been received from listeners during this short time of operation.

When WSY was started, the Birmingham News donated money to help start a station at the Alabama Polytechnic Institute, now known as Auburn University. On February 21, 1923, WMAV went on air.

In January 1925, at the sugges-

Antenna on the roof of the WSY Studio.

tion of Birmingham News Publisher Victor Hanson, Alabama Power donated the WSY equipment to WMAV at Auburn. However, the equipment was already obsolete and of little use to them. Rather than disappoint their supporters, the College's Extension Service and Department of Electrical Engineering voted to purchase a modern transmitter, build two 200-foot towers and outfit a studio on the 3rd floor of Comer Hall. The new station was dubbed WAPI. All stations east of the Mississippi started with the W, and the API stood for Alabama Polytechnic Institute.

WAPI broadcast from Auburn until 1928, when it moved to Birmingham to take advantage of the large population and access to more on-air talent. Their studios were located on the top floor of the Protective Life Insurance Building on 20th street and 3rd Avenue North. Just one block from the last WSY studio at the Loveman's building.

By then, Birmingham had another radio station. Dr. J.C. Bell started WBRC, which stood for Bell Radio Corporation. Both WAPI and WBRC branched off into television stations in Birmingham decades later.

The Alabama Power Company started WSY to stay in contact with their employees in remote locations, but they quickly found they could kick start radio broadcasting in the south. They had the knowledge, they had the money, and they had the power. Pun intended. They also knew when it was time to get out and let others grow radio.

▲ FIRSTS

The Club at the end of the world

The end of the world has come more times than we can count. I am always surprised that doomsday cults can keep recruiting people when their predictions fail time and time again. There have been some serious incidents that legitimately get people nervous about the end of the world. Plagues, pandemics, wars, the list goes on and on. In the late 1990s, we were looking at another end of the world crisis.

It went by many names—the millennium bug, the year 2000 problem, or what most of us called it, Y2K. January 1, 2000, was when the computers were going to rise up and exact their revenge on us.

When early computer programmers wrote a new computer language, they didn't think about what would happen when the calendar went from the 1900s to the 2000s. They did not consider that one day, 19 in the year, would switch to 20. Even our checkbooks at the time had the 19 printed in the date area, so all we

BIRMINGHAM

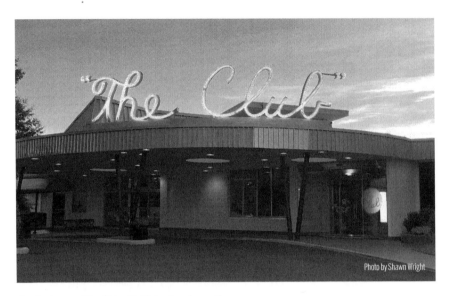

Front entrance of The Club with it's iconic red neon sign.

had to do was think about the last two numbers. Typing in the 19 was not needed for computer programmers, so typing only the last two numbers of the year saved them keystrokes and time.

Only as we got closer and closer to the year 2000 did someone start asking the question, "what's going to happen to the computers when the year 2000 comes around?"

Programmers sprang into action. A lot of time and money went into preparing for the Y2K bug. Computer Code was rewritten for programs that companies had been using for years. Retired programmers made out like bandits when they were enlisted to come back and rewrite the code. They were the only ones that knew how to write these older programming languages, such as COBOL. Younger programmers had never needed to know those languages and wouldn't need to know them in the future.

All sorts of predictions were being made. What was going to happen if we didn't fix it? As with any end-of-the-world type situation, some people got hysterical. People were acting like our personal computers would rise up and become our robot-overlords.

Whenever I think of Y2K or robot-overlords, I think of The Club, a private dinner club located on Red Mountain. The Club was opened in 1947 by Robert S. Smith and a group of investors. Smith, executive secretary at TCI, was in charge of providing entertainment, food and lodging for visiting U.S. Steel executives. He wanted to show the visiting executives the best Birmingham had to offer, and this led to the idea of starting this private dining club.

The original location for The Club was to be on Shades Creek Parkway on the other side of Homewood. Some zoning problems with that location made building there less than ideal. The project architect convinced founder Robert Smith to reconsider the idea of building on the crest of Red Mountain to take advantage of scenic views. In a way, Homewood's zoning laws were a gift for The Club. Today, Robins & Morton currently occupies that land on Shades Creek Parkway, while the Club enjoys a fantastic view of Birmingham instead of a view of the Shell Station.

Growing up in Homewood, The Club was always an enigma to me. The entrance was just off Valley Avenue on the Homewood side of Red Mountain. The large columns and iron gates gave it an air of mystery and exclusivity. You could see the building, perched on the crest of Red Mountain, from downtown Birmingham. My parents were not members, so the opportunity to go there never came up when I was younger.

During the 1990s, I had the opportunity to attend events at The Club. I went to business meetings and wedding receptions there. I even attended a grand gala celebrating Birmingham's participation in the 1996 Olympics.

My wife and I got married on June 19, 1999, and we had our reception at The Club. The wedding date was chosen due to the availability of the ballroom. We were in love and optimistic about the future, even though the end of the world was less than six months away.

Later that year, we attended the annual New Year's Eve celebration at The Club. Our table was located in the ballroom where The Club's older clientele

The view from The Club.

enjoyed celebrating the new year. Sitting amidst the tuxedos and ballroom gowns, my friend said he felt like we were on the Titanic.

We settled into a night of merriment with friends. A big band was playing old standards as partygoers tried to remember how to waltz or do their best imitation of it. Behind the band were four huge numbers, each probably 15 feet tall, that spelled out 2000. About 30 minutes before the stroke of midnight, the last zero fell from its wire. It rolled over in the space behind the band turning 2000 into 200. It was the first sign of the apocalypse.

The drinks continued to flow as midnight came closer. As the countdown to midnight was called out, guests moved towards the large floor-to-ceiling windows that overlooked Birmingham. If you were going to watch the end of the world, there was no better vantage point than The Club on Red Mountain. 5, 4, 3, 2, 1, and nothing.

Nothing happened. No lights flickered, computers didn't rise up and destroy the city, and planes didn't fall out of the sky. Either this preparation and teeth-gnashing were all for nothing. Or what I like to think, everyone had done their job and turned Y2K into a non-event.

The band kept playing throughout the whole thing, just like they did on the Titanic. The party wrapped up, and everyone went home. The year 2000 started just like every other year.

Since 2000, life as we know it has gone on. Since then, there have been events that make Y2K seem a little silly. But at the time, it was all-consuming. Businesses have since turned their attention to the business at hand, and The Club is still serving its noticeably younger members, and my wife and I continue to celebrate wedding anniversaries.

It's the end of the world as we know it, and I feel fine.

The First 911 Call

There are many first calls we can look back to in history. On March 10, 1876, Alexander Graham Bell spoke into his new invention, the telephone, and asked his assistant on the other end, "Mr. Watson—come here—I want to see you."

Almost a century later, on July 20, 1969, Neil Armstrong's first words from the moon were, *"Houston, Tranquility Base here. The Eagle has landed."* When he stepped on lunar soil, he said: "That's one small step for man, one giant leap for mankind."

★ HALEYVILLE

I never understood why Bell would ask Watson to *"come here; I want to see you,"* when what he really wanted was to have a conversation and test out his new invention. Of course, having a phone conversation had never happened before, so maybe he did want him to come to where he was.

Neil Armstrong had a little bit of time to decide what he was going to say when the lunar module

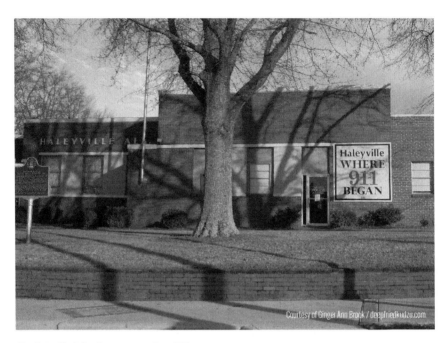

Courtesy of Ginger Ann Brook / deepfriedkudzu.com

The Haleyville Police Department, where 911 began.

landed on the moon and when he took his first step. He knew the significance of his words and that they would be etched in history. Even still, the calm and collected mission commander meant to say, "That's one small step for A man..." He can be forgiven for not saying it, in light of the moment, or maybe he did say it, and it was lost in the miles between the moon and earth. No matter what happened, it gave grammarians and conspiracy theorists plenty of fuel for their fire.

What Alexander Graham Bell gave to us with the phone became indispensable in our everyday lives. If you wanted to check up on a family member in another state, you would write a letter and wait for a reply. With the phone, you place a call and are instantly connected.

If there was an emergency, you could pick up the phone and call the fire station or police department if you had the phone number close at hand. In an emergency, would you display the same calm demeanor as Neil Armstrong? Could you find the number for the fire department or police department? Probably not. And authorities knew this as well.

The first group to raise awareness was the National Association of Fire Chiefs in 1957. They recommended using a single number, around the country, for reporting fires.

It took another decade until the President's Commission on Law Enforcement and Administration of Justice saw that the use of different telephone numbers for each type of emergency was contrary to a single, universal number. They recommended that a "single number should be established" nationwide for reporting emergencies.

Federal Governmental agencies and officials sprung into action in support of this recommendation. The Federal Communications Commission was tasked with developing a solution.

The FCC met with the American Telephone and Telegraph Company (AT&T) to develop a number and implement it quickly. On January 12, 1968, AT&T announced that 911 would be the emergency code in the United States.

For those who are not old enough to have suffered through with a rotary dial phone, let me explain. The larger the phone number, the longer it took for the dial to rotate, and the longer it took to place your call. Dialing a number that started 223 was much more enjoyable than dialing one that began 879. I lived in an 879 neighborhood, so I know the pain.

911 was chosen because it was easy to remember, and even with the initial 9, it made for a quick call. Especially since you didn't have to dial four more numbers. It helped that 911 was not used as an area, office, or service code.

Here is a brief description of the ten-digit phone number you have to dial now. The first three digits are the area code. It used to be just 205 in Alabama, but with more phones available, more area codes have been added for a total of 6 as I write this. The next three digits is the central office code, also known as the exchange code. There are big, windowless AT&T buildings in your area that handled these calls. The last four digits is the line number.

Congress got behind the proposal and passed legislation allowing 911 to be used nationwide as a single number to call emergency services.

The timing was right for this single emergency number. Telephone systems were becoming more and more automated, and because of that, there was less of a need for operators. And since operators handled most emergency calls, routing them to the appropriate agency depending on the issue. Fewer operators meant emergencies were not being handled, and callers would have to search for the phone number they needed, wasting valuable time.

While 911 was a national proposal and would be implemented by AT&T, then the only national phone system. Smaller regional systems outside of the Bell System did not have to implement 911.

Bob Gallagher, president of Alabama Telephone Company, read about the new 911 designation in the Wall Street Journal. He was upset that the smaller carriers were left out of the conversation. But seeing an opportunity, Gallagher decided to beat AT&T to the punch.

He knew they had to act fast, and they chose Haleyville, Alabama, where the companies system was already installed.

An argument was being held across the country about where they would locate the physical 911 phone to receive the emergency call. Should it be at the hospital, the fire station, or the police station? They chose the Haleyville police station, and Alabama Telephone Company employee Bill Frye installed the system in less than a week.

In my mind, I can see the bat phone from the campy 1966 television show Batman. When commissioner Gordan needed Batman's help, he would call Batman on his dedicated phone, which was red and sitting on Bruce Wayne's desk. And that was not far off from reality in Haleyville.

On February 16, 1968, Alabama State Representative and speaker of the house Rankin Fite made a 911 call from the Mayor's office. A red "hotline" phone rang on a dedicated 911 line at the Haleyville Police station. U.S. Congressman Tom

Bevill answered the first 911 call in the United States.

Years later, Representative Bevill said, "I had no idea then that the emergency system would become as big as it has."

After the successful call, everyone celebrated with coffee and doughnuts. Of course they did. It was the police station after all.

Haleyville, Alabama, made the first 911 call. It was a non-emergency call and would happen again and again around the country as more systems came online. Nome, Alaska, was the second to place a 911 call, just six days later.

The day after the historic phone call, they realized they had forgotten all about payphones. Payphones were popular back then, and they cost 10 cents a call. All payphones were modified to make a 911 call without the dime.

Over the decades, 911 has been updated and become a part of our lives. In larger cities, enhanced 911 can identify where a call is coming from and send help if the caller can't provide the information. It's a number none of us want to call but are grateful it is there when we need it.

Haleyville's 911 system is still in operation, making it the first 911 system and the longest-running system in the United States. And if you want to see a little bit of history when you are in the area, the red "hotline" phone is on display at the Haleyville Police Department.

Part 3

THE ATHLETES

Sports are important in Alabama.
They are woven into the fabric of our society.
We play it, we watch it, we bet on it and we obsess
about it. In this section we have stories about high
school football, basketball and the greatest coach
in Alabama history. And we finish with a first in
hockey that happened right here in Alabama.

Bear Bryant wants you to call your mama

I want to tell you about one of the ads produced in this story. It may not be the most successful ad produced by Luckie, but it may be the most talked about. The Bear Bryant Ad for South Central Bell.

From time to time, I read stories on the internet about the commercial, what happened, and how that famous tagline came about. Or what those commenters thought happened. These stories were usually wrong, and credit was given to the wrong people. I wanted to set the record straight, so I talked with the creative director on that project, my dad Leo Wright.

It all starts with an early commercial that Coach Bryant was in. Leo Wright tells the story.

★TUSCALOOSA

"We had done a spot with Coach Bryant for BTNB, Birmingham Trust National Bank, in which he was really acting as a spokesperson, and he was supposed to walk and talk at the same time, go from one place to

another, and sell a credit card, which at the time was a BankAmeriCard. And the coach had problems saying he would say Bank American Card. When we would say, coach, it's BankAmericard, and he would say Bank American Card. But we fixed it in the post."

"So several years later, South Central Bell hired Coach Bryant to be the spokesperson, do several spots for them. And having worked with him before, we knew some of the limitations and things that we wanted to not do with him, which was to make him a spokesperson. We wanted him to be as natural as he could be and make him comfortable. And he wasn't really selling anything. He was just telling us something from his heart."

"And my wife and I were in a supper club at that time, and I was telling the group how we had Coach Bryant and that we need to do some TV spots with him. And we wanted him to be just very natural and be Coach Bryant. And one of the people at the Supper Club was a very loyal and outspoken Alabama fan, Larry Wilson. And Larry said, 'Well, you know, every time a new freshmen class comes in, he has them first thing, sit down and write a postcard home to their mama saying they are okay.' And so immediately that gave me an idea."

"And when I went back into work, I got with our writer Lu Cruce and the art director Randy Sims and told them this little bit. So then Lu took it and put it in context, opening with that and saying how important it was to stay in touch and that, you know, your phone was close by and all you had to do was pick it up and call. And she added, 'have you called your mama?'"

"So we arranged to shoot Coach Bryant in his office in Tuscaloosa, and we hired a production company out of Tuscaloosa, Joe Whigham, who had shot other things with Coach Bryant so he would know how to work with him, too. And everything got set up, and Coach Bryant was very relaxed, and he went through the script, and we all said, That's great, you know, thank you. And he said, 'Would it be all right if I added something?' And you know, who's going to say no to Coach Bryant? And so we said, sure, let's, let's roll it again. And we rolled it again."

"And after the line, 'have you called your mama today?' He added, 'I sure wish I could call mine.'"

"That was a line that we could not have added to it and had it be real. It had to come from him. And it really made the spot and became a very big favorite of not only Alabama fans, but Auburn fans and anybody else who saw the spot."

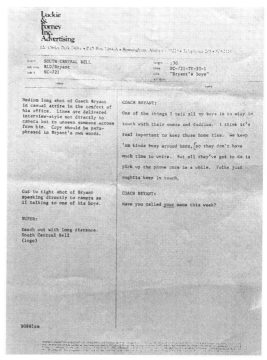

The original script from Luckie & Forney Advertising

If you haven't heard the commercial, the lines that Bear Bryant spoke are:

"One of the first things we tell our players is keep in touch with their families. And when our freshmen first arrive, we ask them to write a postcard home. Right then. You know, we keep them pretty busy, but they always have time to pick up the phone and call. And it's really important to keep in touch. Have you called your mama today? I sure wish I could call mine."

Leo was not finished. "One interesting story was when the people at Bell told us that they had gotten a phone call from a man in Louisiana who said that he had been sitting there watching television. And the spot came on and he thought, you know, I really need to call my mama. And so he gets up and calls her and she died later that night. And he just wanted to call and thank him for prompting him to have one last call with his mama."

"It became very popular. And Lewis Grizzard even wrote a book that said there was called, 'Don't forget to call your momma… I wish I could call mine.' That was a popular book. We did other spots with Coach Bryant at the time, and frankly, I don't even remember what they were. This was the ultimate spot for Bear Bryant and South Central."

So there you have it, the story of the South Central Bell Bear Bryant Ad. Coach Bryant finished his career as head coach at the University of Alabama, South Central Bell became BellSouth, and then AT&T and Luckie continued to do great work.

And since the creative team did such a great job, I wanted to give credit where credit is due. Creative Director is Leo Wright. Lu Cruce is the Copywriter, Randy Sims is the Art Director, and Director/Cinematographer is Joe Whigham of Helios Productions in Tuscaloosa, AL.

If there is one thing we have learned from this short story, make sure you call your momma.

▲ THE ATHLETES

Greenville Basketball

This story is about Marion Ramsey McQueen, known as M.R. McQueen on papers, Mac to his friends, and just plain ol' granddad to me. He was also known by the name Skeeter, named by a traveling salesman who happened to see the tall, gangly child and said, "that boy looks like a 'skeeter." For those of you who are confused. A 'skeeter is a mosquito. At least he looked like one to that salesman. Later on, it was shortened to Skeet.

Skeet was born on September 3, 1904, and grew up in the sleepy town of Greenville, Alabama. A farmer's son and one of eight children, the McQueen's had lived in Alabama's black belt since around 1850.

Greenville was close to the Federal Road that started in Milledgeville, Georgia, and passed through Montgomery, passing close to what would eventually become Greenville on its way to Mobile and finally New Orleans. The road was constructed through the

Photo provided by Rhetta McQueen Wright

The Greenville Basketball Team on the steps of the downtown Birmngham Athletic Club. Marion "Skeet" McQueen is on the bottom row left. Vernon Stabler, bottom row right, would go on to star for the University of Alabama.

Creek Indian frontier to provide ease of movement for federal troops in the lead-up to the War of 1812 between the United States and Great Britain.

Before we start our story, I need to tell you what was happening up north at the end of the 19th century.

On December 21, 1891, in Springville, Massachusetts, James Naismith published rules for a new game called basketball. It was nine versus nine, using a soccer ball and two peach baskets. In 1906, metal hoops, nets, and backboards replaced the peach baskets. The soccer ball was also replaced by a Spalding ball, similar to the one used today. With the help of the YMCA, basketball spread throughout the country.

Thirty years after that first basketball game, Greenville High School's season was just getting started. Sports fans in Greenville knew this team was special and that they would go far. The city council appropriated money to have electric lights on the ball court. Everyone in town went to the games. The talk of the town was that these boys would do them proud.

The enthusiasm paid off when that team was invited to the 1921 state basketball tournament. The newly formed Alabama High School Athletic Association had its first state-wide basketball tournament. And on one of those teams was a gangly son of a farmer known as Skeet McQueen.

When the team boarded the train to Birmingham, the school band and the entire town were there to see them off and wish them well.

My grandfather, who took pride in being thrifty when I knew him as an old man, was given $5 by his father, a lot of money in those days. He came home with $3. Of course, he did.

Most of the team had never ventured far from home and much less spent the night away. Birmingham made a big impression on them. They stayed at the Birmingham Athletic Club and would swim in their large indoor pool.

The Greenville High School team practiced and played their games outdoors, as many teams did at that time. A dedicated gym was just not available everywhere. Playing on an indoor court in Birmingham was a mental and physical test for the team. And imagine what they thought about swimming in an indoor pool.

When telling the story, my grandfather, Skeet, would embellish it with tales of playing with no subs and how they had to have their legs rubbed down between games so that they could continue. He complained about how other teams had multiple changes in uniforms, but they didn't. It was questionable how that made a difference in the game, but it did make for a good story. Even still, there seems to be some truth in these tales.

Left to right: the Southern Club, the Birmingham Athletic Club and the Young Men's Christian Association.

During the first game, against powerhouse Ensley High School, Greenville's star forward, Marion Riley, was knocked out of the game, and since they already had subs in the game, Greenville continued with only four men. Despite this, they went on to win the game 37-26.

Greenville defeated Sidney Lanier in the second game, despite what sports-writers called "a rather rough but not dirty game." Sidney Lanier, the best team in Alabama, was defeated 32-23.

In the third game in 24 hours, Greenville faced Springville High School, a "mediocre team," according to the press. Star forward Vernon Stabler scored 12 points before Springville scored their first. It looked as if Greenville was moving on. But the team was physically falling apart. Stabler was soon removed from the game. Vernon's younger brother was pressed into service and went in as a forward even though he did not weigh over 100 pounds. It was just too much with Stabler and Riley out of the game. Springville clawed their way back and defeated Green-ville 30-14, moving onto the Final Four.

Would this be Springville's Hoosier moment? The one where the underdog school goes on to beat the big city school and win the tournament? Unfortunately no. They lost to mighty Central of Birmingham, who went on to win the tournament.

Greenville High School, the pride of Butler County, only made it to the Elite 8.

After the tournament, Greenville High School principal Mr. C.B. Gamble received a letter from the Birmingham Athletic Club. They praised the players for playing "nothing but sportsmanlike ball and no doubt would have been victorious had not the team been so badly crippled. "The letter also stated that Vernon Stabler was the best individual player in the tournament. It will be remembered that Greenville defeated the fast Ensley and Sidney Lanier teams and was the eighteenth of the twenty-three teams to leave the court.

The team's core went on the following year to make it as far as the Elite 8 and then again in 1925. Vernon Stabler went on to star for the University of Alabama basketball team.

Greenville did not appear in the state basketball tournament until almost 30 years later, in 1964.

After high school, Skeet left Greenville and enlisted in the United States Navy in January 1925, and then spent the next 22 years in service. He saw the world and survived the attack on Pearl Harbor. After the war, he, his wife, and two daughters settled in Mobile, Alabama.

When my mother, as a child, would visit relatives in Greenville during the late 1940s and 50s, she noticed that everyone had the same things hanging on their walls. The free Jim Dandy calendar, some family portraits, a picture of five dogs smoking and playing poker, and a picture of the 1921 team.

My mother was told time and again by relatives or old-timers, "Gal, your daddy played on THE TEAM!"

It was said among family members that Uncle Mott would stand in front of the team portrait and weep after having a little too much whiskey.

That first team to go to the first tournament stayed in the hearts and minds of the people of Greenville who were there at the time. They may not have been the winners of the tournament or even the runners-up, but to the town of Greenville, they were the champions. They were THE TEAM.

◢ THE ATHLETES

Football in the Courts: Homewood vs. Tuscaloosa

In 1974 Homewood High School and its football team were only three years old. The coach was only 26 years old. To think that a team this new, this young, could break into the Alabama State 4A football playoffs was unthinkable. But that was right where they stood after beating rival Mtn. Brook 48-6 to finish with a 9-1 record.

At the end of the regular season, Tuscaloosa High School was declared the Region 7 champions, with a 5-1 regional record, besting Homewood with an identical record. But then Homewood caught a break.

Before the last games of the regular season, the Alabama High School Athletic Association ruled that a player on the Tuscaloosa team was ineligible to play since he was over the age limit of eligibility. The player in question, Elbert Williams, was 19 years old. Tuscaloosa was fined, and they were forced to forfeit their

HOMEWOOD

first game of the season to Holt High School. This ruling was catastrophic for the team. A win over Druid City on the last game of the schedule would have put them into the state playoffs.

The ruling would put Homewood into the playoffs.

Tuscaloosa school officials sprung into action, and attorney Ralph Knowles filed a complaint in the Tuscaloosa circuit court on behalf of the players against the Alabama High School Athletic Association.

Knowles questioned the State Bureau of Vital Statistics saying out of 14 living children in the family, the bureau only had four birth certificates on file. And they said that brother Henry Lee Williams was dead even though he was a Junior at Tuscaloosa High School.

The school, family, and attorneys produced a family bible stating that Elbert was only 18, which was also on his driver's license, social security, and selective service records.

Circuit Judge Fred Nicol ruled that Elbert Williams was 18 and that a new birth certificate be issued.

Athletic Association president Bubba Scott accepted the ruling and ordered that the penalties against Tuscaloosa be rescinded. There was one problem. The board would not meet until Saturday. Williams was not eligible to play on that Friday night game against cross-city rival Druid City. The last regular-season game of the year.

If using a birth date in a bible as "proof" confuses you, the bible has been used for generations to record family events: marriages, births, baptisms, those types of things. The family bible was passed down from generation to generation. Before recording vital records was mandatory, this was the only way to keep track of family vitals. It was essential when families had to "prove" these events when trying to secure benefits like military pensions.

Or for keeping your child eligible to play football.

With this ruling, Tuscaloosa was back in the playoffs after their win against Druid City, knocking Homewood out.

Homewood principal Michael Gross lawyered up and sprung into action with the support of the Homewood Board of Education. They filed in Jefferson County circuit court, and judge William Thompson declared Homewood the champions instead of Tuscaloosa.

With a stalemate and the first-round playoff games fast approaching, the case was going to the Alabama Supreme Court. The Alabama High School Athletic Association asked the supreme court to set aside both court rulings and let them make the final ruling, which is precisely what the Alabama Supreme Court did.

The Athletic Association went back to its original decision. Tuscaloosa would have to forfeit a game making Homewood the region champions.

But the drama was not yet over.

At the same meeting, Tuscaloosa principal Doug Killough accused Homewood of playing an ineligible player all season and that they should forfeit their games.

The player in question was Taylor Wingo. He had transferred from Ramsay High School, where he played the year before. Ramsay is just over Red Mountain from Homewood in the Birmingham city limits.

Homewood must have known this was coming because they produced a stack of affidavits claiming that Taylor Wingo was perfectly eligible. The athletic association said it would "duly investigate" the charge. Accusations were dropped, and Homewood was ready to face their first-round opponent.

The Homewood team spent that week practicing to play a team that they didn't know if they would get to play. Homewood's coach, Alvin Bressler, had them ready to go.

Often, the winner in a competition is the team that handles adversity the best. Before Dothan and Homewood played in the finals, they both faced adversity. Dothan had a bye in the first round, but they won in overtime against Murphy 10-7 in the quarterfinals. They beat West End in overtime 21-20 in the semifinals, placing them in the finals against Homewood.

Homewood had a more difficult route to the championship. In the first round, they got their revenge on Hueytown 21-14, the only team that beat them during the regular season.

In the quarterfinals, they faced favorite Banks High School. It wasn't a matter

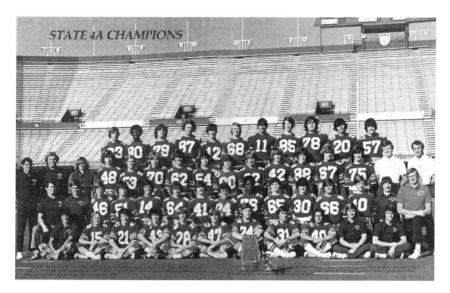

Homewood High School Patriots. The 1974 State 4A Football Champions.

of who played in the playoffs but who would have the privilege to get beaten by Banks.

Banks was undefeated, leading up to the second to the last game of the year against local-rival Woodlawn. This match was the high school game of the century, pitting Banks All-American Quarterback Jeff Rutledge against Woodlawn All-American Running Back Tony Nathan. Both would be playing for Bear Bryant the following year. The game was played in front of 42,000 fans at Legion Field. Banks won the game 18-7. The following week must have been a letdown as they lost their last match 34-27 against West End. No slackers themselves, West End finished undefeated on the way to the playoffs.

Banks was looking to bounce back after a week one bye. A Montgomery sports writer predicted the game against Homewood to be a thrashing 28-14 in favor of Banks. Either Banks couldn't bounce back, or they underestimated the upstart Homewood team. It had been three years since Banks had been shut out, almost as long as Homewood was a school. Homewood won 12-0.

Homewood moved on to the semifinals to play the team that was supposed to challenge Banks, Anniston High School. Homewood dispatched them 18-0 on the way to the finals.

Homewood faced the Dothan Tigers in the finals, led by junior phenom Steadman Shealey and running back Greg Ramsey. A few years later, these names would be called out at stadiums in Tuscaloosa and Tallahassee. It was a tough game fought at Birmingham's Legion Field.

On the last play of the game, with Homewood leading by 3 pts., Dothan quarterback Steadman Shealy passed to a wide-open Greg Ramsey in the endzone for the game-winning touchdown. The ball slipped through Ramsey's fingers and fell safely in the end zone. This night, there was no overtime miracle for Dothan, and Homewood won 10-7.

Both teams had challenging games and oversized opponents on their way to the championship, but Homewood played the biggest game of all. Against an unknown opponent, before they could even start their playoff run, they first had to win in the courts.

■ THE ATHLETES

Gordie Howe
Scores A Goal

H ockey came to Birmingham, Alabama, in 1976. Nobody was surprised; well, everyone was surprised. Alabama in the 1970s was much better known for its collegiate football teams, stock car racing, and the heat. It seemed like an odd fit for a sport generally played in the colder climates of the great white north.

The Toronto Toros of the World Hockey Association was in a losing situation, trying to find fans to attend their games. Making it harder for them, the team shared the city with the mighty Toronto Maple Leafs, who had played there since 1917 and were in the estab- lished National Hockey League.

BIRMINGHAM

The original franchise started as the Ottawa Nationals during the World Hockey Associations' inaugural season in 1972. The first year was a disaster, averaging only 3,000 people a game. They moved the franchise to Toronto and were sold to John Bassett as the majority owner at the end of the season.

Howe scores his 1,000th goal on Bull's goalie John Garrett.

The team tried to win over fans in Toronto for three years, and they had difficulty finding a suitable arena to play in. The lease that they had for the Maple Leaf Gardens was pretty bad. Let's say the owner of the Maple Leafs did not want a WHA team in his city. Bassett decided it was time for a move, and he looked 950 miles south to a city in transition, Birmingham, Alabama.

John Bassett was not unfamiliar with Birmingham. Starting in 1974, he was the owner of the Toronto Northmen of the World Football League, the WFL. Before the season began, controversies forced a move, and they became the Memphis Southmen. Regional rivals of the Birmingham Americans.

Hockey in the American south was pretty unique. At the time of the move, the only teams in the deep south were the Houston Aeros of the WHA and the Atlanta Flames of the NHL. The current crop of southern NHL teams did not start moving south until the 1990s.

I think it's safe to say that the sports fans in Birmingham knew nothing about hockey. But one thing we have learned over the years is that if a new league or sport wants to give it a shot in Birmingham, the fans will support them as long as they put on a good game and win.

When hockey came to Birmingham in the mid-70s, one of the first goals was to teach the fans about the sport. In the first couple of exhibition games, the announcers would describe the rules such as offsides, power plays, slashing, high stick, and other hockey rules. Excitement was building, and four thousand fans showed up for the first intrasquad game.

Another large crowd showed up for an exhibition game against the NHL's Atlanta Flames. A natural rival that could have helped both teams if not for being in different leagues.

The Birmingham Bull's original roster featured players that the fans didn't genuinely appreciate due to our limited hockey knowledge. Frank Mahovolich, The Big M, had scored 561 goals in a career dating back to 1958. He played on six Stanley Cup-winning teams, the Canadian National Team, and was inducted into the Hockey Hall of Fame.

Paul Henderson had a successful career in the NHL before coming to Birmingham. He was a Canadian hero during the 1972 Summit Series. An eight-game series featuring the best Canadian and Soviet players. Henderson scored seven goals in the tournament, including a last-second game-winning goal, winning the series.

And Václav Nedomanský, a former Czechoslovakian player who won a silver and a bronze medal in the Olympics. He was inducted into the Hockey Hall of Fame in 2019. He is best known as the first hockey player to defect to North America just two years before coming to Birmingham. I can only imagine the culture shock Birmingham must have been to him.

The WHA had been cherry-picking big-name players in their quest for legitimacy, such as Bobby Hull, who was in his prime when he joined the league.

One of the biggest names was coming to Birmingham for the regular season home opener on October 8, 1976. The Houston Aeros came to town led by hockey

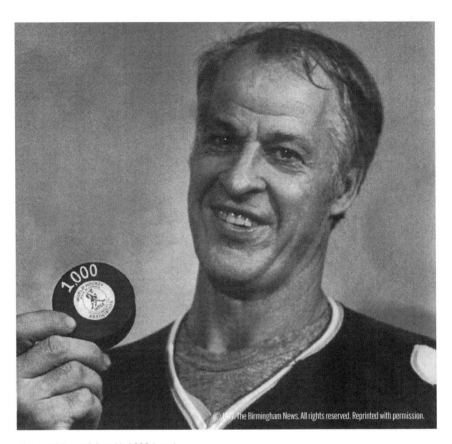

Howe and the puck from his 1,000th goal

legend Gordie Howe. His two sons, Mark and Marty, were featured on the team.

Frank Mahovolich always seemed to be the old man of the team to me because of how long he had been playing professionally. He was only 38 years old, and while old for professional sports, it's not that old. Mahovolich started in 1958, but Gordie Howe made his debut with the Detroit Red Wings in 1946, a full 12 seasons before Mahovolich.

Howe had retired in 1971 after playing 25 seasons, his entire career with the Detroit Red Wings. His #9 jersey was retired the following year. But he wouldn't be retired for long.

A year later, he was offered a contract to play in the new World Hockey Association. The Aeros had signed his two sons to contracts to entice him out of retirement. The opportunity to play with his sons was too much. He joined the team.

After four years in Houston, the Howe family made a move, and they signed with the New England Whalers.

On December 7, 1977, the New England Whalers came to Birmingham for what would turn out to be a special game for Gordie Howe.

Leading up to the game in Birmingham, Howe had been suffering from arthritis, and he had sat out a couple of games. Worst of all, he had been sitting at 999 goals scored for ten games. The near misses and intense games were wearing on his psyche as he was trying to get to that milestone. Howe started the game, and all it took was one minute and 36 seconds of the first period to make history.

10,211 attended the Wednesday night game to cheer on their Bulls and maybe, just maybe, see a bit of sports history. The game started, and after only 11 seconds, Paul Henderson was sent off for tripping, giving the Whalers a powerplay. Bulls Goaltender John Garrett stopped shot after shot. Most of the power play had been burned when the puck passed by Bull's defenseman Dale Hoganson, and Howe put the puck in the bottom left corner of the net.

John Garrett said it best: "...Gordie was standing in front of the net, and the pass came to him, a one-hopper, and he picked it off about three inches above the ice and nailed it. I got a picture of the play with the puck in the net behind me, and Gordie signed it, 'Thanks for all the help!'"

It happened so fast that photos of the goal show Garrett standing up, watching the puck go in. He had no time to react. And like that, John Garrett, who would go on to be one of the best goalies in the game, became the answer to a trivia question. "Who did Gordie Howe score his 1,000th goal on?"

Gordie Howe's goal sparked his teammates, and the Whalers led 5-1 at the end of the second period before finishing the game 6-3.

After the end of the game, Gordie Howe said it best, "Thank God it's over! I'm a lucky boy. All my dreams have been answered."

At this game, Gordie Howe had played professional hockey for 32 years since he first suited up for the Detroit Red Wings. He was 49 years old.

Two years later, the NHL expanded to include some teams from the WHA. New England was in, and Birmingham was out. Detroit still had rights to Howe, but they let him stay with the New England Whalers. He played one last season, and at his last game, he was 52 years and ten days old, making him the oldest man to play in the NHL.

Retirement always seemed to be a problem for Gordie Howe, and in October 1997, he signed with the Detroit Vipers of the IHL to play one last game. This game allowed him to play a professional game in each of six decades. He was 69 years old.

Publicity stunt or not, it was a remarkable feat. 20,182 fans came to honor Howe, and he received a standing ovation before the start of the game. He played two shifts and was almost credited with a goal after a shot by Brad Shaw deflected off his shin and nearly went in the net.

After the demise of the WHA, Birmingham fielded a team in the Central Hockey League for the next couple of years. They have existed in name for the past couple of decades and currently play in the Southern Professional Hockey League, playing in Pelham, a suburb to the south of Birmingham.

Gordie Howe passed away on June 10, 2016. He gave so much to hockey and gave so much to those who were lucky enough to watch him play.

Just like John Garret, Birmingham would go on to become the answer to a trivia question. "Where did Gordie Howe score his 1,000th goal?" Nowadays, most people would probably guess a lot of hockey towns before they would ever guess it was the Football Capital of the South, Birmingham, Alabama.

Part 4

ALIEN ENCOUNTERS

Our journey to the moon would not have happened
if not for the people of Huntsville, Alabama. But
before we could send men and women to space, we
needed to send a monkey first. In this section, we
tell about Miss Baker going to space and we tell
about alien objects coming from space to Alabama.
And because we love to tell a good story, we will
learn about a famous director and his story about
aliens kidnapping a small child.

▲ ALIEN ENCOUNTERS

The Sylacauga Meteorite

Sylacauga is known for many things. Most famously for its fine white Madre Cream marble, which is used in buildings worldwide. In Washington D.C. alone, it has been used in the Lincoln Memorial, the Washington Monument, the U.S. Supreme Court building, the state of Alabama Capitol, and the State Archives in Montgomery.

And Sylacauga is known as the hometown of television star Jim Nabors, better known to all of us as "Gomer Pyle."

But this is not about one of those Sylacauga stories.

I was first introduced to Sylacauga, Alabama, in the pages of the *1974 Guinness Book of World Records*. A prized possession of my childhood. It was a thick book filled with oddities, freaks, record-breakers, and ordinary people. And ordinary people like Ann Hodges from Sylacauga.

This is her story.

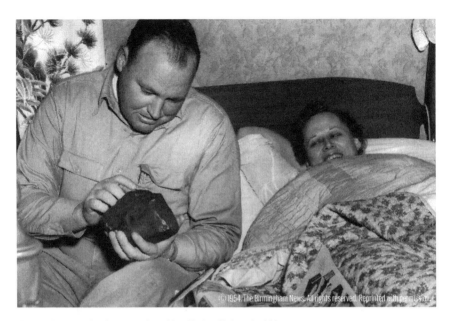

Eugene Hodges holds the meteorite at his wife, Ann Hodges, bedside.

It was Tuesday, November 2, 1954, about one o'clock in the afternoon. Ann Hodges was not feeling well, so she rested on the living room sofa. She was covered in two thick quilts to keep her comfortable. Her mother was there at the house helping out.

The skies over central Alabama were clear. A slow-moving fireball appeared in the southern sky. The following sonic boom nearly knocked a boy off his bicycle in Montgomery, Alabama. The fireball fragmented.

People reported seeing "a bright reddish light, like a Roman candle trailing smoke." Others saw "a fireball, like a gigantic welding arc," with tremendous explosions and a brown cloud. Reports came from as far away as Birmingham, Atlanta, Columbus, Montgomery, and Greenville, Mississippi.

Some people thought there was a plane crash, and since it was the height of the cold war, some thought it could be the Soviet Union or maybe even a UFO.

Authorities searched for a crash site over a three-state area with as many as 40 planes taking part. But no reports of missing planes came in.

One of the rocks from the fireball headed towards a field, and the other headed straight towards the home of a tree surgeon, Eugene Hodges, and his wife, Ann.

Ann slept on the sofa, and her mother was sewing in the next room. There was a mighty crash, and the house filled with dust. Ann lept to her feet, and her mother ran into the room, thinking the gas heater had exploded. As the dust cleared, they noticed the hole in the roof, and the pain in Ann's side disclosed a large bruise.

The larger of the two rocks, weighing in at 8.5 lbs, came through the roof, grazed the couple's Philco console radio, and hit Mrs. Hodges as she slept beneath two quilts.

They looked for answers and discovered a rock on the floor. They immediately called the police and fire departments. A local geologist came by to check out the rock, and he was the first person who identified it as a meteorite.

Eugene had no clue that anything had happened until he got home at the end of the workday and had to push his way through the crowd to get to his front door. "We had a little excitement around here today," Ann told him. "A meteor fell through the roof."

Due to all the excitement and attention, Ann was admitted to the hospital the next day. She told the Associated Press. "I haven't been able to sleep since I was hit," Even though the bruise was impressive, she was not seriously hurt by the meteorite.

With Cold War paranoia running high, the Sylacauga police chief confiscated the black rock and turned it over to the Air Force, who flew in by helicopter to take it to Maxwell Air Force Base.

As soon as the meteorite was gone, the Hodges wanted it back.

Adding to the confusion, the Air Force had it, and the mayor promised it to the Museum of Natural History at the University of Alabama. Why he thought he had a right to promise it is unclear.

Hodges said, "I am going to demand that the Air Force return the stone to me.

Attorney Hugh Love (left), Ann Hodges, and the Director of the Alabama Museum of Natural History Walter B. Jones (right).

They had no business taking it away in the first place."

While trying to decide his next move, Hodges looked at the hole in his ceiling and declared: "I think I could get enough evidence that the thing fell in my house."

The Air Force identified the rock as a meteorite and then sent it to the Smithsonian Institute, which was thrilled to receive it. When asked for it, they refused to send it back to Alabama. It took Alabama Congressman Kenneth Roberts to intervene and have it returned.

Birdie Guy wanted the meteorite as well. You see, it fell on her property. The Hodges were renting her house, and according to the law, it was rightfully hers.

"Suing is the only way she'll ever get it," Ann Hodges said, "I think God intended it for me. After all, it hit me!"

Birdie Guy intended to sue for the meteorite, and Ann Hodges was going to countersue for her injuries. Cooler heads prevailed, and the case was settled out of court with the Hodges offering Birdie Guy $500 for the meteorite. Eugene tried finding a buyer for it but failed. The excitement of the event had worn off. He missed his moment. He used the meteorite as a doorstop before eventually donating it to the Alabama Museum of Natural History.

But what about that other piece of the meteorite?

A farmer named Julius Kempis McKinney found the smaller piece on his property a few miles away. This one weighs 3.75 lbs. He was driving a mule-drawn wagon when the mules would not continue due to a black rock in their path. He pushed the stone out of the way, and they continued.

That night, after hearing about Ann Hodges's experience, he retrieved the rock and took it home. McKinney connected with a lawyer to help sell the piece of the meteorite that he had found.

Later reports indicated that he made enough money from the sale to buy a house and a car. Eventually, that meteorite was donated to the National Museum of Natural History.

Getting hit by a meteorite made Ann Hodges a minor celebrity. Her photo appeared on the cover of *Life* magazine's December 13, 1954 edition with an article entitled, "A Big Bruiser From the Sky."

She was also a guest on Gary Moore's TV quiz show, *I've Got a Secret*, to reveal her secrets, and she was the front cover story in almost every major magazine.

All the national attention took its toll on Ann. She suffered a nervous breakdown, and her health grew worse. The marriage collapsed in 1964, and she died of kidney failure in a nursing home at the age of just 52. Eugene figures all the attention took it out of her, and she never did recover.

According to my *1974 Guinness Book of World Records*, Ann Hodges was the only person to be hit by a meteorite. Since then, a couple more have come to light. They aren't as dramatic as the one that hit Ann Hodges.

In 1992 a boy in Mbale, Uganda, was hit in the head by a 3-gram fragment of a meteorite after bouncing off a banana tree.

In 2009, a 14-year-old German boy, Gerrit Blank, was hit in the hand by a pea-sized meteorite. While he wasn't seriously injured, the rock did leave a scar and scared him. It hit him hard enough to knock him off his bike and bury itself into the road.

And back In 1972, a meteorite killed a cow near Valera, Venezuela. A farmer and doctor found the cow and didn't think much of the incident. They processed and ate the remains of the cow. They kept some fragments of the meteorite, selling them years later.

In 2018 the meteorite that hit Ann Hodges took flight once again. The Paris Museum of Natural History asked to borrow the meteorite for their "Meteorites from Sky to Earth" exhibit.

Transporting the rock was no small task involving appraisals, insurance, a special container, and a team of fine art couriers to get it to Paris for an eight-month exhibit and then back to Tuscaloosa.

Not bad for a rock that was once a doorstop.

■ ALIEN ENCOUNTERS

Able and Baker in Space

Alabama is lucky to have its share of astronauts born in Alabama or lived here for a time. Henry Hartsfield, James Voss, Mae Jemison, Kathryn Hire, and Kathryn Thornton are some who were born here. There are more who have lived in Alabama, specifically Huntsville, while working for NASA and preparing for missions. There is a chance you could have run into an astronaut in Alabama. It is slim but still a possibility.

There is a better chance you ran into a Monkey-naut if you lived in Alabama. I met my first and only monkey-naut at the U.S. Space and Rocket Center in Huntsville in the 1970s. My grandparents lived in Decatur, a short drive from Huntsville, and the Space and Rocket Center was a great thing to do while I was there. My elementary school class also took a class trip there.

Growing up in Birmingham, most schools did the

Miss Baker poses on a model of the Jupiter vehicle, May 29, 1959.

school-trip trifecta of the State Capital in Montgomery, Moundville in Tuscaloosa, and it wouldn't have been complete without the trip to the U.S. Space and Rocket Center in Huntsville.

But back to my brush with fame. On my trips to the Space and Rocket Center, I would visit with Miss Baker, who lived in a glass-enclosed display amongst the space hardware and science exhibits. The first time I saw her, she had been in retirement for over a decade.

At the beginning of the space programs in the United States and the Soviet Union, animals were used as test subjects to determine the effects of space flight and weightlessness before they sent humans into space.

In 1947, Fruit flies were sent into space on a recovered V-1 rocket to study the effects of radiation.

The first mouse went into space in 1950, and many tortoises, frogs, spiders, fish, nematodes, and tardigrades have made the flight over the decades.

The Soviet Union sent some dogs into space. The best known was Laika in

1957, who died just five hours into the flight.

Monkeys had flown as early as 1948. For over a decade, those flights failed. And later, apes had flown successfully.

Miss Baker and her flight companion Able were two of the most notable monkeys to fly.

Able was a seven-pound rhesus monkey born in Independence, Kansas. Officials stressed her place of birth because rhesus monkeys are revered by some people in India. They wanted to make sure everyone knew Able did not come from India.

Baker, better known as "Miss Baker," was a one-pound squirrel monkey. Miss Baker was born in Peru in 1958 and was purchased by NASA from a Miami pet store along with other monkey-naut candidates.

The United States had flown monkeys and mice by Aerobee rocket to heights below the edge of space beginning in 1951. Outer space does not have a definitive altitude above the Earth's surface. But 100 km or 62 miles above sea level is the Kármán line, which is recognized internationally as the beginning of space.

To make it into space, NASA moved to the larger Jupiter missile, and on December 13, 1958, Gordo, a Navy-trained squirrel monkey, was on board when the rocket launched. It is believed that Gordo survived the flight, but the nosecone he was in sank in the Atlantic and was never recovered.

Five months later, on May 28, 1952, Able and Miss Baker were launched from Cape Canaveral, Florida, and rode in a Jupiter missile to a height of more than 300 miles. During the 1,500 mile flight, they reached speeds of 10,000 mph and experienced 9 minutes of weightlessness.

I would like to imagine that our two friends were busy floating around the capsule, flipping switches, and looking out the window during this time of weightlessness, wearing tiny silver astronaut suits. But unfortunately, no. They were strapped in tightly to custom-made harnesses that monitored their vitals throughout the flight.

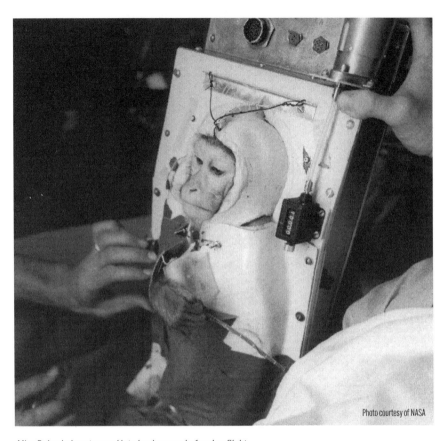

Miss Baker being strapped into her harness before her flight

After a 16 minute flight, they splashed down in the Atlantic ocean, not too far from Puerto Rico.

This trip is remarkable from the missions before because our monkey-nauts survived the flight.

And they were not the only ones on the flight. They were accompanied by Neurospora, human blood samples, e.coli, onions, mustard and corn seeds, yeast, and sea urchin eggs and sperm.

Think about it. This mission was two years before any humans flew into space, and they became major celebrities. The reporters jostled to get closer during a post-flight press conference, but the monkeys calmly munched peanuts and crackers. They even appeared on the June 15, 1959, Life magazine cover.

Unfortunately, it's not all good news. Four days after the flight, Able died from a reaction to anesthesia while they were removing electrodes used to track vitals.

Miss Baker went to live at the Pensacola Naval Air Station. Scientists wanted to know if the ride in the rocket would have any effect on Miss Bakers' offspring, so they searched for a suitable spouse. They found one in a monkey they called Big George. They married in 1962.

Wouldn't you have just called him a mate? Why would they need to have a wedding? A keeper was "determined that they should not live together in sin while on public display."

Miss Baker's popularity was consistent over the years. She appeared on over 20 network shows, including *Mike Douglas*, *Good Morning America*, and the *Dinah Shore Show*.

In 1970 The U.S. Space & Rocket Center opened in Huntsville, Alabama. The center was opened just after the Apollo 12 moon landing, while interest in the space program was at its peak. The museum has over 1,500 artifacts, including a Saturn V rocket. The center was about to get the only living space artifact.

In 1971, Miss Baker and her husband, Big George, made the move to Alabama.

She would receive between 100 and 150 letters every day from children worldwide.

On January 8, 1979, Big George died. Officials didn't want Miss Baker to be lonely, so they found a suitable mate in Norman from the Yerkes National Primate Research Center. Three months later, Miss Baker and Norman wed in a ceremony presided over by Alabama District Court judge Dan McCoy.

There was a little wedding drama. She refused to wear the white wedding train provided for her, tearing it off after a few seconds. Who can blame her?

A few years later, Miss Baker became sick, and she was sent to the Auburn University School of Veterinary Medicine for treatment. She passed away from kidney failure in 1984 at the age of 27. Norman moved back to live the rest of his life at the Yerkes National Primate Research Center.

Not only was she one of the first two monkeys to survive a space flight, but she was also the longest-lived squirrel monkey on record.

After her death, Miss Baker returned to the U.S. Space and Rocket Center. She was buried on the grounds next to her first husband, Big George. Over 300 people attended her funeral, and when you walk past her tombstone, from time to time, you will find that someone has placed a banana on top, a fitting way to honor this space legend.

But what about Abel, her crewmate who died four days after the mission? Yeah, things didn't go so well for her. She was stuffed and placed back in her flight harness. She is periodically displayed at the Smithsonian Institute in Washington, D.C.

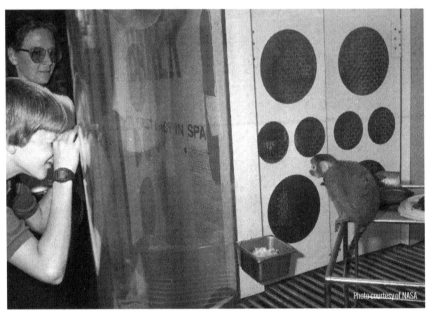

Miss Baker, a squirrel monkey who made a historical flight aboard the Jupiter (AM-18) in May 1959, is seen here in her viewing area where she resided at the U.S. Space and Rocket Center.

Stars Fell on Alabama

Have you ever heard the phrase "Stars Fell on Alabama?" Of course, you have. If you grew up in Alabama, you can't avoid it. You probably can't remember the first time you heard it, but it has always been around.

Maybe you first heard about it when you watched the movie *Stars Fell on Alabama*, which opened in theatres (or video on demand) in 2021. This rom-com starred James Maslow and Ciara Hanna. It's about a Hollywood agent who returns to his hometown of Willow Springs, Alabama, for a high school reunion. He brings a friend to pretend to be his girlfriend, and I am sure you can figure out where the plot goes from here.

Maybe you first saw the phrase when it was used as a slogan on Alabama license plates, replacing "Heart of Dixie" as the primary slogan, which has been used for years.

On September 4, 1951, Alabama lawmakers passed

legislation requiring that a heart and the phrase "Heart of Dixie" be included on all Alabama license plates. Bill Spoor, Birmingham advertising man, proposed the slogan. The idea was that people around the country would see the slogan, want to vacation, and spend their money in Alabama. And if they didn't know where the state was, the tag told them it was in the heart of dixie.

Here's a side note. The word dixie comes from $10 notes issued as currency in Louisiana before the civil war. Each note bore the word dix, French for the number 10.

Over the decades, with the word dixie falling out of favor and the legislature making it impossible to remove, the slogan became smaller and smaller.

In January 2002, the phrase "Stars Fell on Alabama" was added to the tag, making the Heart of Dixie slogan smaller and pushed to the corner. "Stars Fell on Alabama" stayed on the plates until 2009.

Maybe you first heard about stars falling on Sylacauga in 1954. Actually, it was just one meteorite. It came through the roof of the Hodges home and landed on Ann Hodges as she napped on the sofa. We talked about her during season 1 of the Alabama Short Stories podcast.

The first mention of the phrase "Stars Fell on Alabama" was in a book of the same name, published in 1934 by Carl Carmer. Carmer had taught English at the University of Alabama in the 1920s and wrote a book of essays. Stories he had collected from his travels around the state. Oral histories are passed down in families, such as a night when stars rained down on Alabama.

In a way, it is remarkable that Carmer stayed long enough to write the book, much less travel to all corners of the state to research the folklore that Alabama presented him. After arriving in Tuscaloosa, Carmer, a New York native, was warned by a new colleague "...if I knew you well enough to advise you, I'd say, 'For God's sake, get out of here before it's too late.'"

More than likely, you know "Stars Fell on Alabama" by the song of the same name.

A famous depiction of the 1833 meteor storm, produced in 1889 for the Seventh-day Adventist book Bible Readings for the Home Circle. Adolph Vollmy in 1889.

The first one was written in 1934, not long after Carmer's book was published. It is a jazz standard composed by Frank Perkins with lyrics by Mitchell Parish and more than likely took the name from Carmer's book, much to his chagrin.

One of the earliest popular recordings of "Stars Fell on Alabama" was recorded on August 27, 1934, by the Guy Lombardo Orchestra, with brother Carmen Lombardo on vocals. It was soon followed that year by Richard Himber and his Ritz-Carlton Orchestra.

Over 100 artists have recorded the song. Among them are Bing Crosby; Ella Fitzgerald; Louis Armstrong; Cannonball Adderley; John Coltrane; Bob Dylan; Jack Teagarden; Jimmy Buffett; Billie Holiday; Anita O'Day; Dean Martin; Frank Sinatra; Doris Day; Frankie Laine; Art Tatum; Erroll Garner; Kate Smith; Mel Torme; Ricky Nelson; Stan Getz; Harry Connick Jr.; Sonny Stitt; and Lizz Wright.

Taylor Hicks, Birmingham-born and bred musician and winner of Season 5 of American Idol, sang a version for the "Stars Fell on Alabama" movie soundtrack. Of course, he did; who better to do it.

The Marching Southerners of Jacksonville State University in Jacksonville, Alabama, perform the tune at every home football game and exhibition. The song has become the unofficial anthem of both the Southerners and Jacksonville State University.

But what do stars fell on Alabama mean?

It was a Wednesday morning in November 1833, and for those awake early enough in Alabama, they were to witness a remarkable phenomenon. Stars started to fall in the sky.

It had been a clear and cool night, and while meteors were not uncommon, this morning was exceptional. Thousands of meteors were shooting across the sky, radiating out from a center point.

The Florence Gazette wrote:

The scene was as magnificent as it was wonderful. To the eyes, it appeared to be in reality a "falling" of the stars; as we heard one describe the scene, "it rained stars."... *The meteors succeeded each other in quick succession until the dawn of day: presenting a remarkable scene of nocturnal grandeur, which may be more readily conceived than described.*

Not everyone took to this celestial display with the same awe. Some in Huntsville, many of those slaves, were seen shouting and praying, thinking that the judgment day had come. Not everyone saw it that way. Native Americans saw the meteors as a sign of good luck.

Across the country, others reacted to it differently. The Cheyenne nation established a peace treaty, and the Lakotas reset their calendar. It was noted by historical figures such as Harriet Tubman, Frederick Douglass, and Abraham Lincoln. Joseph Smith, the founder of the Church of Jesus Christ and Later Day Saints, watched it with his followers along the banks of a river. They had been driven from their homes by anti-Mormon settlers, and Smith believed this was "a literal fulfillment of the word of God" and a harbinger of the imminent second coming of Christ. People around the world reported the meteor shower.

What those people saw was not the judgment day; it was the Leonids.

As we now know, the Leonids are a meteor shower associated with the comet Temple-Tuttle. And little did the people of 1833 Alabama know, but Temple-Tuttle was a periodic comet and would be coming back 33 years later.

I mentioned earlier that the meteor shower radiates from a center point in the sky, and that center point was located in the area of the constellation Leo. Hence we get the name Leonid.

Let me try and explain what is going on as simply as possible. As comet Temple-Tuttle approaches the sun, solid particles, known as meteoroids, are ejected from the comet as frozen gases evaporate. Earth passes through this stream of meteoroids, and that is how we get the Leonid shower.

One estimate of the peak rate of the 1833 shower was over one hundred thousand meteors an hour, but another estimate said it was more than 240,000 meteors during the nine hours of the storm. No matter how you look at it, it was not a small shower. The intensity of the storm has stood out in the minds of those watching and who would tell their story to future generations.

Stars falling on Alabama was either a terrifying or awe-inspiring event in 1833. A century later, the tale was told by Carl Carmer. The song "Stars Fell On Alabama" tells of a different type of event. Of a couple kissing in a field of white and seeing stars. As the song ends:

"My heartbeat like a hammer, my arms wound around you tight
And stars fell on Alabama last night."

Close Encounters in Mobile

When I was growing up, my grandparents lived in Prichard, Alabama, and they eventually moved to Eight Mile, which, as the name tells you, is eight miles from Mobile. This was in the 1970s, and there was not much in Eight Mile in the eyes of this youth. I haven't been there in decades, so things may have changed, but at the time, it seemed as if there were only open lots, long-vacant roads, industrial fencing, and Mobile College. I am not sure if it was planned, but it seemed only fitting that my grandparents, the good Baptists they were, would move right down the road from the Southern Baptist-affiliated, University of Mobile, as it is now known.

I turned 16 years old in 1979, and the year before, my grandfather was teaching me how to drive on the roads of Eight Mile. As a man who survived Pearl Harbor, he was utterly unfazed that his life was in my hands. We were driving on one of those long-

★ MOBILE

vacant roads when I noticed a chain-link fence. Behind it was large white boxes or pods stacked on top of each other. They looked out of place, and they seemed very familiar.

These boxes were white. The bottom and top edges on the front and back were beveled, and a large open window extended the length of each box. Each box had blue and red stripes on them.

They looked so out of place, and then it hit me. These looked like they came from the movie *Close Encounters of the Third Kind.* In the scene where the scientists met the aliens. These pods were control towers placed around the edge of the alien welcome center constructed at the base of Devil's Tower in Wyoming.

This movie was fresh in my mind, having seen it recently in the theater. Close Encounters was released in 1977 and was a huge success. It was written and directed by a young Stephen Spielberg, fresh off his blockbuster movie Jaws. And it starred Richard Dreyfuss, who incidentally was in the movie Jaws. Dreyfuss had heard all about the film during the filming of *Jaws* and campaigned hard to get the starring role, eventually convincing Speilberg to cast him.

John Williams wrote the soundtrack and the iconic five-note score that became synonymous with the film. He had written the score for *Jaws* and *Star Wars*, released the same year as Close Encounters. And I bet you can hear the music from the opening credits playing in your head right now.

But why would those props be in, of all places, Mobile? I never went back to see if those pods were from the movie, but what else could they be, and who would have them shipped from Hollywood to sit in a lot outside of Mobile? I went on with my life, but I never forgot those pods.

The story of *Close Encounters of a Third Kind* follows Roy Neary, an Indiana electric lineman who has a close encounter with a UFO and how it changes his life. UFO researcher J. Allen Hynek categorized the levels of encounters with a UFO in his 1972 book *The UFO Experience: A Scientific Inquiry*. A close encounter of the first kind is when a person witnesses an unidentified flying object. A close encounter of the second kind is when there is some interference with a vehicle or electrical device. Maybe someone has a physical reaction to this close encounter. Scorched earth or affected vegetation would be of the second kind. The third kind is where an alien is present. Roy Neary gets to experience all three types.

The majority of filming would take place in Burbank, California, and Mobile, Alabama. And no one was more surprised than the citizens of Mobile. There are a lot of places in the US that filmmakers could have chosen, but none of them had two enormous, empty plane hangers like those at the closed Brookley Air Force Base in Mobile. There was not a studio large enough to contain the UFO mothership planned for the movie's final scene. Native Californians descended on Mobile to experience what summer heat was all about in 1976.

Mobile officials and citizens were baffled by the attention their city was receiving, but they were thankful. Unemployment was at an all-time high. Mobile was a center for World War II production and employed thousands of people. Once the war ended, the jobs went away, and the area suffered from high unemployment. The newly created United States Air Force took over Brookley Field in 1947 and became an important economic engine for the region. My grandfather, who I

Clapper board from the movie "Close Encounters of the Third Kind."

mentioned earlier, worked at Brookley after retiring from the Navy.

Unfortunately, good things come to an end, which came via retribution from President Johnson. In the 1964 Presidential election, Alabama citizens voted for Barry Goldwater, and Johnson punished the state by closing Brookley Air Force Base. Incoming President Richard Nixon confirmed the base's closure to save money due to the Vietnam War. The base was finally closed in June 1969.

Hollywood actors such as Melinda Dillon, Teri Garr, Francois Truffaut, and Bob Balaban starred with Dreyfuss, but local actors also appeared. Locals were used as extras throughout the movie. They were aboard trains at a train station in Bay Minette and in the alien encounter scene at the movie's end. The small aliens that descended the spacecraft ramp were played by young girls wearing alien costumes from a Mobile dance company. Some locals even had minor speaking parts, like Mary Gafrey, who played Roy Neary's next-door neighbor, Mrs. Harris.

While everyone did a great job, none stood out as much as Cary Guffey, a child actor from Douglasville, Georgia. Cary was just three years old and turned four during production. He played Melinda Dillon's son, who aliens abducted. Guffey was a natural talent and would deliver a great performance in just one or two takes. Anyone who has had a three-year-old child should be blown away by this. Maybe it's just me, but I couldn't get my three-year-old to pose for a picture, much less do multiple takes in a movie.

So, where are they now? Spielberg wrote and directed some of our favorite movies from the past three decades. Richard Dreyfuss and the other actors would continue to do outstanding work. Bob Balaban is in almost every movie I watch. He is everywhere. Google his name; you will know him.

Cary Guffey would be cast in movies and TV, last appearing in the miniseries *North and South* in 1985. He would leave acting at the ripe old age of 12. After high school graduation, Guffey would attend the University of Florida and then Jacksonville State University, where he earned his MBA. He is a financial planner with PNC Investments in Birmingham, Alabama.

Movie aliens came to Mobile and Brookley field in 1976, but a quarter of a century earlier, Brookley had its own encounter of the first kind. Between 1950

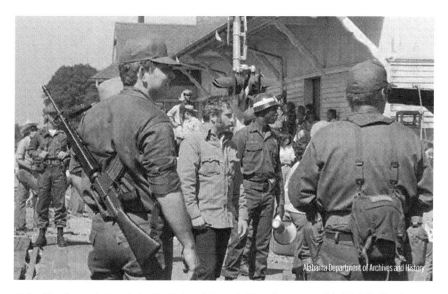

Richard Dreyfuss and extras during the filming of the movie "Close Encounters of the Third Kind" at the railroad depot in Bay Minette, Alabama.

and 1954, a series of UFO sightings prompted the air force to open Project Blue Book and investigate these and other occurrences around the nation. The August 28, 1952 sighting was noteworthy because it was confirmed on radar. Something was there; they just don't know what.

Hollywood coming to Mobile was a good thing for everyone involved. Soon after, the Mobile Film Authority was created to liaise between the film industry and the local community. Seeing a good thing, the Alabama Film Office was established so the rest of the state could take advantage of film productions looking for a great place to film. *Close Encounters of the Third Kind* were nominated for an Oscar in nine different categories at the 1978 Academy Awards. The film would win two Oscars for Best Cinematography and Sound Effects Editing. Richard Dreyfuss and John Williams would also win Oscars that year. Dreyfuss was best actor for *Goodbye Girl*, and Williams ran against himself and won for the original score for *Star Wars*.

Today Brookley Field is home to the downtown Mobile airport and Airbus, where they assemble and deliver Airbus commercial aircraft worldwide. When they cleared the hangers after Hollywood left town, items were sold to locals as scrap and as movie memorabilia. And those boxes, the pods I noticed in Eight Mile? Those were props from the movie.

Part 5

EXCEPTIONAL PEOPLE

Alabama has no shortage of extraordinary people.
The stories we have chosen to highlight include
someone who has risen to one of the highest-
ranking offices in government and one who lived on
the fringes of Birmingham society. We feature
a musician, a pilot and a man who honored
a relative by building a wall.

■ EXCEPTIONAL PEOPLE

William Rufus DeVane King - Alabama's First Vice President

Every four years, citizens in our country go to the polls to vote on a presidential candidate. Each vote also includes a vote for a vice president running with the presidential candidate as well.

Franklin Roosevelt's first vice president, John Nance Garner, famously said the title is "not worth a bucket of warm spit." It's a role that has always been up for interpretation throughout White House administrations, with the VP ready to step in or step back, whatever the case may be.

John Adams, our very first vice president, called it the most insignificant office ever the invention of man contrived or his imagination conceived. In his case, it was the bitter consolation prize. You see, he came in second place in the race for President. And that was how we chose the vice-president at that time.

For much of our history, vice presidents had no specific constitutional duty except to cast tie-breaking

William Rufus King 1939 portrait

votes in the U.S. Senate.

A vice president is often chosen to balance out a ticket. Not because they have a great relationship with the presidential candidate. Some Presidential candidates may have only just met their party's Vice-Presidential candidate when they received their party's nomination. It can make or break a campaign or be as insignificant as some earlier vice presidents considered their role. No matter how they got there or what kind of relationship they have with the President, they are a heartbeat away from the presidency.

Consider these incidents where a vice-president became President.

In 1841, William Henry Harrison died just 31 days into his presidency. He was just the ninth President, and there was a brief constitutional crisis because United States Constitution did not fully define some aspects of presidential succession. Congress cleared things up, and vice-president John Tyler was sworn in as President.

In 1850, Zachary Taylor served just 16 months before he died suddenly of a digestive ailment. Taylor's presidency was described as a "more forgettable president than a failed one." His Vice-President, Millard Fillmore, was sworn into office.

In 1865, Abraham Lincoln was assassinated, and Andrew Johnson became President. Lincoln chose Johnson because he was from the south, and he wanted to show a message of national unity. Johnson favored quick restoration of the seceded states to the Union without protection for the former slaves, contrary to what Lincoln had fought the war over. It just goes to show that choices do matter.

In 1881, another short-term President, James Garfield, was assassinated after only four months in office. Garfield did not die from his gunshot wounds but the infections caused by his doctors. Vice President Chester A. Arthur was sworn in and served the rest of the term.

In 1901, William McKinley was assassinated at the beginning of his second term. Vice-President Theodore Roosevelt succeeded McKinley as President.

In 1945, Franklin D. Roosevelt was serving in the middle of his fourth term as President when he died. It was at the end of World War II, and Roosevelt was in failing health. He was at the Little White House in Warm Springs, Georgia, where he had gone to gain strength for an upcoming event. While sitting for a portrait, he slumped forward. His doctor diagnosed a massive intracerebral hemorrhage. He died later that day. Vice-President Harry S Truman was sworn in and was expected to lead the United States to victory over the axis powers.

In 1963, John F. Kennedy was assassinated in Dallas, Texas, and Lyndon Baines Johnson was sworn in as President.

In all incidents of a Vice President succeeding the President while in office, it was because of a death. But in 1974, Richard Nixon resigned in disgrace because of the Watergate scandal, and Vice-President Gerald Ford was sworn in as President. A month later, Ford issued Proclamation 4311, which gave Nixon a full and unconditional pardon for any crimes he might have com-

William Rufus King etching

Engraving of Chestnut Hill, published following King's death in the Illustrated News, New York, April 30, 1853. The house was destroyed by fire during the 1920s.

mitted against the United States while President. Ford did not retain his office in the next election.

Some Vice-presidents have succeeded the President they served under through the election process. The last vice president to become President was George H.W. Bush, who succeeded Ronald Reagan in 1988.

Alabama had its share of vice presidential candidates.

John Sparkman had served for nine years in the house of representatives and was a Senator when Adlai Stevenson tapped him to run as the Democratic Party's nominee for Vice President in 1952. Stevenson and Sparkman would be defeated in the general election by the Republican candidate Dwight D. Eisenhower and his vice-president Richard M. Nixon. Sparkman would continue to serve in the senate until 1979.

If the Stevenson/Sparkman ticket had won, Sparkman would have been the second United States Vice President from Alabama. The first was William Rufus King in 1853.

William Rufus King was born in North Carolina in 1786. The son of a Revolutionary War Veteran, King was educated in private school and attended the University of North Carolina. He left before he graduated to pursue the study of law and indirectly learn the ways of politics, which is where our story is headed.

After serving in the North Carolina House of Commons, King was elected to the U.S. House of Representatives from North Carolina and served three terms.

King always dreamed of traveling outside the United States and was able to do so when in 1816, he was appointed to the staff of William Pinckney, who was the new U.S. Minister of Russia and the Kingdom of the Two Sicilies. After his position ended, King traveled throughout Europe, returning home in late 1817.

While he was gone, the Alabama and Mississippi territories saw a land rush as settlers searched for good farmland. In the years before King left for Russia, Andrew Jackson had fought the Creek Indians in the Alabama territory, effectively taking control of their land. This action enabled more and more people to move into these territories safely.

King joined the migration in 1818 and purchased land on a bend in the Alabama River in Dallas County, known as "Kings Bend." He developed a large cotton plantation run by slave labor, and he called the plantation "Chestnut Hill."

He may have operated a plantation, but his career in politics was not over. He was a delegate to the Alabama convention, which organized the State of Alabama in 1819, and he wrote much of the original constitution of Alabama. The state legislature elected him as the United States Senator. He served there until 1852 except for serving two years as United States Minister to France during President James K. Polk's term in office.

James Buchanan and William Rufus King had an unusually close relationship. As bachelors serving in the government in Washington, they lived together for 13 years until King's death. There was even talk about them running together as President and Vice-President. They got the opportunity at the 1852 Democratic National Convention (held in 1851).

King supported Buchanan to be the presidential candidate, but it wasn't to be; Franklin Pierce of New Hampshire was nominated on the 49th ballot. To appease the south, William Rufus King was selected as the party's vice-presidential candidate on the second ballot.

Franklin Pierce won the general election, but King came down with tuberculosis during the campaign. He traveled to Cuba in hopes that he could regain his health in the tropical climate of the Caribbean. On March 4, 1853, he was not in Washington to take his oath of office. By a special act of Congress, he was allowed to take the oath outside the United States, the only one ever to do so. He was sworn in outside Matanzas, Cuba, on March 24, 1853.

Soon after, he traveled back to his plantation at Chestnut Hill, and he died two days later, on April 18, 1853. He was initially buried in a vault on his plantation but was moved to Selma's Old Live Oak Cemetery. Selma was not an unusual location. Selma, which was incorporated in 1820, was planned and named by William Rufus King, whose plantation is just outside Selma.

King never carried out the duties of his office and never presided over a legislative session. President Pierce never nominated another candidate for vice president. The office stayed vacant until John Breckenridge was sworn in with King's friend and roommate, President James Buchanan, in March 1857. After King's death, Buchanan described him as "among the best, the purest and most consistent public men I have known."

William Rufus King, the first and only United States Vice President from Alabama.

The Wichahpi Commemorative Stone Wall - Tom's Wall

I first learned about the Indian tribes in Alabama during elementary school. In fourth grade, we learned the state's history from the book *Alabama Mounds to Missiles* by Helen Morgan Akens and Virginia Pounds Brown. I enjoyed it so much that my parents gave the book to me as a gift for Christmas that year. We learned that the main tribes in Alabama were the Creek, Cherokee, Choctaw, and Chickasaw. In class, their land was outlined over a map of Alabama to show where each tribe lived.

★ FLORENCE

That year, my class visited Moundville on the Black Warrior River, located outside Tuscaloosa, and we learned about the Indians who lived there over 500 years ago. But as fourth graders, we were more interested in running up and down the steep mounds and being away from school for the day.

The Trail of Tears story was given its own chapter in the book, but the tragedy and horror of that time

Photos courtesy of the Florence-Lauderdale Convention & Visitors Bureau

did not register with me until many years later. If I had to guess, it might have been when I realized that the names of towns around the state were Indian names. Towns with names such as Loachapoka, Eufaula, Attalla, Oneonta, Opelika, Tuscumbia, and Wetumpka, to name just a few. In contrast to these towns, you will find Fort Deposit, built during the Creek Indian War, and Fort Payne, in Northeast Alabama.

US Army Major John Payne built Fort Payne (the fort, not the city) to intern Cherokee Indians until they could be forcibly removed in the 1830s to Indian Territory in Oklahoma during what is called the Trail of Tears.

Many Indians died on the way to Oklahoma. They traveled on foot, as much as 12 miles a day, and carried their possessions with them. When moccasins wore out, they went barefoot. When it got cold, they had to make do with what they had. Many did not finish the trip to Oklahoma. The trail of tears behind them was marked with the graves of the old, the sick, and the unfortunate who died along the way.

There was one Indian tribe that we did not learn about in fourth grade called the Yuchi tribe. The Yuchi historically lived in the eastern Tennesee river valley before migrating south to Alabama, Georgia, South Carolina, and some even as far as the Panhandle of Florida. While the Indian removal act of 1830 targeted Cherokees, other tribes were targeted as well. The Yuchi were removed to Oklahoma.

Tuscumbia native Tom Hendrix heard stories about Indians when he was growing up. His stories did not come from a sanitized schoolbook. The stories he was told as a child came from his grandmother.

Hendrix's grandmother told him stories of a teenage girl named Te-lah-nay who lived along the singing river, or Tennessee River as we know it. It was called that because her tribe, the Yuchi, and other tribes who lived along the river, believed a woman lived in it and sang to them.

When authorities came to round up the Indians, they scattered and tried to avoid detection. Te-lah-nay's grandmother put her and her sister in a canoe and sent them downstream. This small action probably saved their lives. When the girls returned, they found graves covered with stones. They guessed that their grandmother had buried those that had been killed. The girls took stones from the river and added them to the graves to honor their ancestors.

The girls continued to evade capture until they were found in a root cellar during mopping up operations by the troops. They were given identification numbers engraved on a metal medallion with the number on the front and US on the back. Te-lah-nay was given number 59, and her sister was given number 60. The soldiers did not know what tribe they belonged to, so they were placed with the Muscogee Creek.

They and the other Indians were forced to walk to Oklahoma along the trail of tears. When she got there, she listened for singing waters and found none.

She knew she would die if she did not get back to her home. After one winter in Oklahoma, she set off on an arduous journey that would take her five years before she made it back to her singing river. She brought a journal of the adventures she had undertaken and the metal tag with the number 59 on it. She kept this

because she thought her name had been changed by the soldiers and would need it when she got back to her homeland.

These stories told to Tom Hendrix by his grandmother had extra meaning for him. You see, Te-lah-nay was Hendrix's great-great-grandmother. His grandmother was passing the stories of her family to ensure that the family legacy would not die.

By the 1980s, Hendrix realized he wanted to learn even more about Te-lah-nay, the Yuchi tribe, and how he could honor his great-great-grandmother and her journey.

He took a trip to Oklahoma and met an elderly Yuchi woman who still knew the language. Her name was Minnie Long, and she was able to interpret the written stories for him. Hendrix told her that he wanted to do something for his great-great-grandmother. "Like a memorial?" She said. "We shall all pass this Earth; only the stones will remain. We honor our ancestors with stones. That's what you should do.'" Hendrix had a plan; he would build a memorial to his great-great-grandmother. Minnie Long changed the course of his life.

In honor of Te-lah-nay, he would lay a stone for every step she took. When he told his wife of his plan, she said if he was really going to do it, he should make it fun. He needed to weigh his truck empty at the cotton mill and then fill it with stone level to the top and weigh it again. She would keep up with the loads he hauled. She predicted 4 million pounds of stone in 1980. By 2011 his wall contained 8.5 million pounds of stone.

When he finished working on the wall, he liked to tell others that he wore out three trucks, 22 wheelbarrows, 2,700 gloves, three dogs, and one old man. There is a stone from every state of the union and 127 countries and territories in the wall. Not to mention a meteorite, a tooth from a t-rex, and the world's largest arrowhead.

Photos courtesy of the Florence-Lauderdale Convention & Visitors Bureau

For 33 years, Tom Hendrix worked on the Wichahpi Commemorative Stone Wall. It is a dry stack wall and is the largest unmortared wall in the United States. The wall is a mile long and snakes around Hendrix's property in Lauderdale County, close to the Natchez Trace. The wall is a very spiritual place for many who visit.

After walking the length of the wall, a spiritual man named Charlie Two Moons told him: "The wall does not belong to you, Brother Tom. It belongs to all people. You are just the keeper. I will tell you that it is wichahpi, which means 'like the stars'. When they come, some will ask, 'Why does it bend, and why is it higher and wider in some places than in others?' Tell them it is like your great-great-grandmother's journey, and their journey through life — it is never straight."

Of the approximately 80,000 Indians removed to Oklahoma, Te-lah-nay is the only one that was proved to have returned to Alabama. Despite the fact that it was a hangable offense to do so. The call of the river was that strong.

"She did not make an ordinary journey; I did not build an ordinary wall," said Tom Hendrix.

For more information about Te-lah-nays journey, you can read about it in the book *If The Legends Fade* by Tom Hendrix.

The Wichaphi Commemorative Stone Wall is located close to the Natchez Trace at 13890 County Road 8, Florence, AL 35633.

Fess Whatley

One of the most popular songs of the early 1940s was Tuxedo Junction. It was initially composed by Erskine Hawkins and members of his orchestra, William Johnson and Julian Dash. When the song was released, it became a huge hit, climbing to number 7 on the charts. Soon after, the publisher requested lyrics. Lyricist Buddy Feyne met with Hawkins, and when he found out what Tuxedo Junction meant, the words came quickly.

Once lyrics were added to the original instrumental score, "white" bands added it to their playlist. The most prominent artist was Glenn Miller. Miller recorded it in 1940, and it soon became a Billboard Number 1 song. His version of the song is noticeably slower than Hawkin's instrumental.

Erskine Hawkins and his band were at a recording session in July 1939, and they needed one more song. He asked for half an hour, and Hawkins, Johnson, and

John T. "Fess" Whatley

Dash got together, took a head arrangement that the band had played before, and Johnson wrote out an arrangement that the band followed for the recording. A head arrangement is a piece of music usually made up during a performance and played by ear.

After they recorded the tune, Hawkins needed a name for it. His valet suggested that he call it Tuxedo Junction, close to where Hawkins lived.

Tuxedo Junction is in the Ensley neighborhood of Birmingham, Alabama, located between two streetcar lines. It was a convenient place for workers from the local mills to get together. "The Junction," as it was known, was the only place for the black community in the area to go listen to live music, go dancing, go shopping, or for a night out on the town. Many performers got their start on the second floor of the Belcher-Nixon building located at the junction. Performers like Erskine Hawkins.

Hawkins started to learn music when he attended the Tuggle Normal and Industrial Institute and joined the band. He tried different instruments before settling on the Trumpet. His real education began when he went to Birmingham's Industrial High School. He played in the band directed by famed music educator John T. Whatley, better known as "Fess" Whatley.

John Lewis Whatley was born in rural Tuscaloosa County, but the family moved to Birmingham so John and his brother Edward could attend the Tuggle Institute. The Tuggle Institute was created to teach African American students printing, woodworking, and industrial arts.

During Whatley's time at the school, trumpeter Sam "High C" Foster was hired to start a band program. A first for African American students in the area. Foster's music program offered an opportunity to learn formal music training. Whatley learned a trade at the school and how to read music. Foster profoundly impacted him and the direction his life would go in.

Whatley graduated from Tuggle Institute in 1913, and he replaced Foster as band director. He held the position for the next four years until he was hired to teach printmaking at Birmingham's Industrial High School in 1917. While there, he organized a parade band, concert band, and eventually a dance band.

In 1924 a new school was built to take its place and is now known as A.H. Parker High School.

Whatley was given the name John Lewis Whatley when he was born. He changed his middle name to Tuggle in honor of school founder Carrie Tuggle's husband, John. The nickname "Fess" came early in his teaching career, which is short for professor.

Whatley was a taskmaster. He was a strict and demanding bandleader, and he required all his musicians to be able to read music fluently. Because of this, his music program became one of the best in the region, and he was widely recognized as a leading music educator.

Not only did he teach printmaking and music, but he performed as well. He

Whatley's SaxoSociety Orchestra in the mid-1920s. Whatley is on the far left with a trumpet.

formed The Jazz Demons, Birmingham's first African American dance orchestra. He didn't have to look far for quality musicians. He filled the band with current and former students. They traveled throughout the country.

As music styles changed, so did his orchestra. His next one was the Sax-O-Society Orchestra, which started in the mid-1920s and was then renamed the Vibra-Cathedral Orchestra in the 1930s. This ensemble was considered the epitome of big band sound of the time.

Alabama State Teachers College President Harper Councill Trenholm was a friend of Whatley's. Trenholm asked him and fellow music educator Len Bowden to help student Paul Bascomb start a band at the college. They established the 'Bama State Collegians. Whatley encouraged his high school students to attend the school and to apply for scholarships. The school would later be called Alabama State University.

The 'Bama State Collegians toured the country and quickly gained a national reputation. Proceeds from their tours helped keep the school from closing during the depression of the 1930s. Erskine Hawkins was one of those collegians who had transitioned from Fess Whatley's instruction at Parker High School to Alabama State. His first two records were billed as Erskine Hawkins and his 'Bama State Collegians. When he changed the name to Erskine Hawkins and his Orchestra, it was filled with those same musicians.

Fess Whatley would train musicians that would populate some of the biggest bands led by leaders such as Duke Ellington, Lucky Millinder, Louis Armstrong, Skitch Henderson, Lionel Hampton, Fletch Henderson, Billie Holiday, and Bessie Smith.

His students would go on to have distinguished individual careers. Two of the most famous are Herman Blount, who would go by Sun Ra, and standup bassist Cleve Eaton. Eaton would work with countless musicians over the years, including Count Basie and the Ramsey Lewis Trio, which included future Earth, Wind, and Fire leader Maurice White on drums.

I was lucky enough to have Cleve Eaton and his band play at my wedding reception which would have been a highlight of my life if not for the fact that I had married the love of my life only hours before.

In 1956 Fess Whatley retired from being an active musician, and he gave Jay Sims of The Huntsville Mirror this quote:

"I love music and probably always will, but I think it is time I quit active

Whatley is known for his music education, but he was hired as a print shop teacher. This is the Birmingham Industrial High School printshop and that may be Whatley in the top right corner viewing a students work.

participation and let the other boys carry on. But before taking a final bow, I would like to offer sincere thanks and appreciation to all those people who represented the clubs, fraternities, sororities, and all other social organizations. For it was they, who came from all walks of life and all races, and allowed me the opportunity to let me play my music, I would not have that wonderful feeling of having rendered a service to those people."

Fess Whatley would retire from Parker High School in 1963, and he died in January 1972. He is buried at Birmingham's New Grace Hill Cemetery.

When we think of jazz or big band music in Birmingham, our thoughts always turn to Erskine Hawkins and Tuxedo Junction. Next time you hear it, and you should play Hawkins' instrumental, remember the people behind the scenes who taught Erskine Hawkins, Sun Ra, Cleve Eaton, and many others not only how to play their instruments but become experts with them. People like Fess Whatley.

Ruth Elder, Pilot

Alabama has a strong history of aviation. Starting soon after the Wright Brothers first powered flight on December 17, 1903. In 1910 the brothers opened a flight school on an old cotton plantation outside Montgomery, Alabama. The operation was short-lived, but the area was used as an airplane depot during World War 1 and then became Maxwell Field.

Maxwell Field, now known as Maxwell Air Force Base, was named in honor of William Calvin Maxwell, born in Natchez, Alabama. He was an ROTC student attending the University of Alabama when the U.S. entered World War 1. He dropped out and joined the Army. He was stationed in the Philippines after the war when he died trying to land his plane. His commander lobbied the Army to name the field in his honor.

We have heard stories about the heroics of The Tuskegee Airmen, and we have heard about many other pilots and astronauts with Alabama roots. Still, I want to focus more on women aviators from Alabama in this episode of the Alabama Short Stories podcast.

There is Katherine Stinson, who was born in Fort Payne, Alabama. She became the fourth woman to earn the FAI pilot certificate. The FAI is the world governing body for air sports. Stinson was the first female pilot to fly a loop, the first female to fly for the U.S. Mail Service, and the first female to fly in Canada and Japan.

Mildred Hemmons Carter was born in Benson, Alabama, and was one of the first women to earn her pilot's license as part of the Civilian Pilot Training Program. Her

National Air and Space Museum, Smithsonian Institution.

license also gave her the distinction of being the first African-American female pilot in Alabama. She was attending Tuskegee University, and she worked in an office that processed applications for the training program. She applied herself only to be rejected because she was not yet 18 years old. She applied the following year again and was accepted.

Mildred met and married Herbert Carter, who was at Tuskegee training to be a pilot, one of the Tuskegee airmen. She applied to be part of the Women Airforce Service Pilots, the WASPS but was turned down because of her race. She became a member of the Civil Air Patrol in Alabama but was denied the opportunity to patrol the state due to her race. In 2011, Carter was declared an official member of the Women Airforce Service Pilots and a Designated Original Tuskegee Airman.

One woman who did become a member of the WASPs was Nancy Batson Crews. She earned her private pilot's license and her commercial pilot's license in 1940. In the spring of 1942, she made her instructor's rating, and that fall was one of the first women to be accepted for the experimental Women's Auxiliary Ferrying Squadron, also known as the WAFS. The WAFS, an awkward acronym, would become the WASPs the following year. Nancy Batson, as she was known during the war years, became the first Alabama woman to fly military aircraft.

Alabama natives Jan Davis, Kathryn Thornton, Kay Hire, and Mae Jemison all became astronauts, traveling to space on the space shuttle. Mae Jemison was the first African-American woman to fly into space.

And then there is Ruth Elder.

Ruth Elder was born on September 8, 1902, in Anniston, Alabama, one of six children of James and Sarah Elder. She entered a short-lived marriage when she was 20 years old. She divorced and then married Lyle Womack when she was 22. I am not sure how and when the two would have met. Lyle grew up in the Panama Canal Zone and attended Iowa State University. No matter how, they married in Birmingham and eventually moved to Lakeland, Florida, where Elder would find work as a dental assistant. Womacks business would have him travel back and forth from Panama.

One day at work, Elder was looking out the window, and she noticed a plane fly past and land in the field across from her office. The man flying that plane was George Haldeman, who had caught the aviation bug a decade earlier and had become an instructor. Ruth Elder soon became his student.

The 1920s was when pilots wanted to become known for a first. The first to fly across the country, the first to fly in the winter, those sorts of firsts. But no first was more desired than New York to Paris.

Charles Lindbergh was an obscure U.S. Air Mail Pilot when he decided to try

National Air and Space Museum, Smithsonian Institution

for the Orteig Prize. A $25,000 reward was offered to the first aviator to fly non-stop from New York City to Paris or the other way around. He completed the feat on May 21, 1927, and became world-famous overnight.

As sure as Elder knew that she wanted to fly, she also wanted to become the first woman to fly across the Atlantic.

Investors were found in Wheeling, West Virginia, who saw an excellent opportunity to cash in on the female Lindbergh. They purchased a Stinson SM-1 Detroiter, a plane capable of an Atlantic crossing and with many similarities to Lindbergh's Ryan NYP. It was named "The American Girl," and the name was emblazoned in script on the sides of the plane so everyone would see.

Elder was given a choice of pilots to fly with her, but Ruth chose George Haldeman. Her instructor and friend, with who she had the most faith.

Her husband had been supportive of her flying but crossing the Atlantic in a plane bothered him greatly. Not only because he cared about his wife, but his manliness was being called into question. He thought he had talked Elder out of her flight when he set off for a short trip to the Panama Canal. Elder had other plans.

Elder and Haldeman traveled to New York to start their trip across the Atlantic. They made a stop in Wheeling, West Virginia, to thank their investors. Elder was swarmed by the press and fans when they got to Roosevelt Field in New York, all wanting to see the female Lindbergh. Elder took to the attention and admiration as if she was born to it.

If you follow any stories about adventurers, you would know that attempting records in the winter is always a bad idea, especially when it is attempted in the North Atlantic. Winter was fast approaching, but Elder and Haldeman ignored the potential for bad weather. They couldn't wait until spring. Several other women were planning flights, and Elder had to be first.

Lindbergh's route was north along the coasts of Maine, Nova Scotia, and Newfoundland before crossing the Atlantic. The American Girl would fly south of that route, keeping them out of the worst weather and closer to shipping lanes.

American Girl lifted off in poor weather on October 11, 1927, and within hours, they ran into heavy storms and would fight them for the rest of the trip. Haldeman had to dump gasoline to keep the plane in the air at one point in the flight. They had been in the air for 28 hours when the engine started leaking oil.

It took Lindbergh 21 hours and 40 minutes to get to Paris, so Elder assumed she could make it in the same amount of time. The French press knew when she was leaving, and they didn't expect her to make it in that time, but by October 13, they wanted to know what happened to the American Girl and its female pilot. Concern for her and her co-pilot George Haldeman was splashed across newspaper headlines.

The oil leak couldn't be fixed in flight, so Haldeman asked Elder to start looking for ships. They were going to have to ditch the plane. Within a few hours, she saw the Dutch oil tanker Barendrecht. They flew over and got the attention of the ship's captain before Handleman brought the plane down for a water landing as close as they could to the vessel. They climbed out on the wing and waited to be rescued by the lifeboat, and just in time. Soon after they were aboard the Barendrecht, the American Girl exploded and sank. The ship set a course for the Azores Islands to drop them off. They eventually made it to France, but this time by boat and military plane.

Ruth's family had been nervously waiting in Anniston, Alabama, for any news about the flight. They had been waiting at a newspaper office, wondering what had happened. They realized that their daughter should be in Paris already, and no one had heard anything. The anxiety was crushing. Her mother sobbed with joy when word finally made it to Anniston that she was safe. "I knew Ruth would be found safe," her mother exclaimed. Her husband wiped away the tears as the rest of the family's fear turned to happiness.

Even though the flight ended short of its goal, the pilots were treated as heroes in France. They made it back to New York City on November 11 and were given a ticker-tape parade. Our pilots then attended a luncheon hosted by Calvin Coolidge at the White House.

Anniston Mayor Sidney Reaves declared December 20, 1927, "Ruth Elder Day." Alabama Governor Bibb Graves enthusiastically endorsed the celebration. He and his entire staff attended. He also ordered the 40-piece National Guard Band of Gadsden to attend along with the pursuit planes of the 108th Observational Corps from Birmingham.

Publicly, Lyle Womack supported his wife and her adventure, but he did not take it well in the background. He especially bristled at being called Mr. Elder or Mr. Ruth Elder by the press and fans.

There would be many opportunities for Ruth Elder following her flight. The admiration, opportunities, and being away from home took their toll on her marriage. While I suspect the marriage may have been on shaky grounds before the flight, it was too much for Lyle Womack's frail male ego. He wanted out of the marriage.

Elders' Stinson SM-1 Detroiter, a plane with many similarities to Lindbergh's Ryan NYP.

According to Womack, one of the reasons he demanded a divorce was because she would not stay home. Also, her failure to kiss him upon returning from her ill-fated flight was cited as a cause of embarrassment. About his divorce, he said, "Ruth chose a career rather than be a housewife, and I have no other course."

The marriage was dissolved just before Womack traveled as a member of Commander Richard E. Byrd's 1929 Expedition to the South Pole. Womack would be an explorer, a lion tamer, and meet his untimely demise when he was kicked by a pet donkey later in life.

The year after Elder's failed attempt, Amelia Earhart became the first woman to cross the Atlantic by plane as part of a crew (she kept the flight log). And on May 20, 1932, five years to the day of Lindbergh's flight, Earhart would become the first woman to fly solo across the Atlantic ocean.

Elder might not have become the first woman to fly from New York to Paris, but at the time, it was the longest flight ever made by a woman, and they established a new over-water endurance flight record of 2,623 miles.

Ruth Elder was cashing in on her newfound fame, and she moved to Hollywood. She became an actress and appeared in the silent movies *Moran of the Marines* in 1928, *The Winged Horseman* in 1929, and *Fashion News* in 1930. Her movie career was over by then, but she continued to fly and participate in air races.

Elder had fame and fortune, but she could not hold onto either. She would tell reporters, "The money slipped through my fingers."

She was in a rough place in 1955 when she met Howard Hughes. He was an aviator himself; he had known about Elder in her early flying days. There was also a rumored relationship between the two. Knowing she needed work, he suggested she apply for a position as a secretary at Hughes Aircraft. He wrote YWH for "You Will Hire" at the top, ensuring she would get the job.

Elder would continue to be interviewed over the years, and the Associated Press wrote a story about her at Hughes Aircraft. She is quoted as saying: "I just love being a working girl." The accompanying photo of her at her desk seems to say otherwise.

Ruth Elder would be married six times. Husband Ralph King would be numbers four and six. They would be together until her death on October 9, 1977. Two days shy of the 50th Anniversary of her flight.

Lou Wooster

For the last couple of years, the people of Birmingham and Alabama have been dealing with the Covid-19 pandemic. It's not the first disease that has swept through Alabama, and it certainly won't be the last. We don't even know if Covid-19 is over just yet. Time will tell.

Our citizens have battled yellow fever, polio, the Spanish flu, and various other diseases over the centuries. But nothing had hit Birmingham as hard as the cholera epidemic in 1873.

Let's set the scene. Birmingham, Alabama, had only become a city two years earlier. City services were still being developed, such as water and sewer. Residents of Jones Valley, where Birmingham is located, had a couple of options to receive water. A couple of miles north of the city is Village Creek. A reservoir was created there to supply people with a sanitary water source. Along the base of Red Mountain to the south

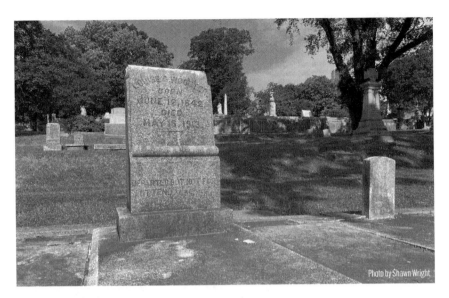

Lou Woosters grave at Oak Hill Cemetery in Birmingham.

were several public wells and springs. These were in the lowest areas of the valley, so when it rained, water would run down from higher elevations, making the groundwater less than sanitary.

The poorest part of Birmingham was Baconsides, where impoverished African Americans lived in huts on a hill above a marshy area. The area is just north of 2nd Ave. North and to the west of where the Innovation Depot is now located. Residents had sunk barrels into the marsh to collect rainwater. When rains would come, filth from the houses would wash down the hills and into the marsh, contaminating their water supply.

Cholera first came to Birmingham by a man only known as Mr. Y, who had moved from Huntsville. He had been in Birmingham for six weeks before his bedding finally arrived. Three days later, he showed symptoms of cholera and died soon after. While it was suspected it may be cholera, the cause of death was not identified, so the proper disposal of the body for a cholera victim was not adhered to. It was assumed that Mr. Y did not become sick until his bedding arrived from Huntsville, which had been going through an outbreak of cholera as well.

When I say properly disposed of, I mean that the bodies of cholera victims would be disinfected with carbolic acid and buried, and bedding and clothing would have been burned.

Less than a week later, two sisters died of the disease. They lived on a hill just above Baconsides. Do I need to tell you that their bodies and clothing were not properly disposed of? It is thought that their body fluids contaminated the water in Baconsides. Cholera spread like wildfire in that community, and according to physician Mortimer Jordan, Jr., every house in Baconsides had at least one fatality due to cholera.

Then the disease spread to the rest of the community. That summer, 128 people died. It might not seem to be that many today, but Birmingham only had 4,000 citizens. By the end of summer, half the citizens would move away to escape the disease.

The Montgomery Advertiser reported: "Families have been leaving here all day by every available means. Stores are closing up generally. Even the drinking saloons are shutting their doors. One drug store has closed and several hotels and boarding houses."

Another newspaper report said: "All are leaving who can, and no business is being done except at Drug Stores and by Physicians."

Some people stayed in town to help, including many of the city's doctors. There were individuals such as city alderman Francis P. (Frank) O'Brien, who became so sick it was assumed he was about to die. A casket was ordered, and the local paper prematurely printed his obituary.

And then there were the prostitutes.

Louise Catherine Wooster, better known as Lou, was born in Tuscaloosa, Alabama, in 1842, and the family moved to Mobile a few years later. Her father died when she was seven and her mother when she was fifteen. Her family was ripped apart. Her two younger sisters were sent to the Mobile's Protestant Orphan Asylum, and Louise went to New Orleans to live with a married sister. Another older sister became a prostitute.

Before her death, Wooster's mother had begged Lou not to let her younger sisters be committed to an orphanage. Lou assumed that would never happen and was surprised when it did. Within a few years, she returned from New Orleans with a forged letter and got her sisters released from the orphanage. They fled to Montgomery and moved in with a family friend. Following in the footsteps of her older sister, Lou entered a Montgomery brothel.

In the early 1870s, industrialists flooded into Birmingham to profit from the area's iron ore. They were followed by rich men looking to make money and poor men looking for work. Lou saw an opportunity, and she moved to Birmingham. She moved just in time for the cholera epidemic and was one of the prostitutes who cared for the sick and helped prepare the bodies for burial.

Half the population had left Birmingham that summer, and once cholera had left, it was replaced by a national economic depression. By the end of the decade, the city had only grown to 3,086. By 1890, the population had grown to 26,178. That is when Birmingham took off.

After the epidemic, business was slow, and Lou had to leave the city. She moved back to Montgomery but returned to Birmingham as people returned to the city.

In 1884 she bought a two-story building on Fourth Avenue North between Nineteenth and Twentieth Streets. She eventually purchased the building next door and lived in one, and operated her brothel out of the other. What was unique about this location was that it was across the street from the Birmingham City Hall. It may seem like a risky location, but she was close to influential men, saloons, and hotels. She was very close to the police, which probably kept her more unruly clients under control. She had the cooperation and protection of Birmingham Police, worthy of her high-class status as a madam.

After the epidemic, physician Mortimer Jordan, secretary of the Jefferson County Medical Society, submitted a paper about the outbreak in Birmingham as part of a larger national paper. As he closed his report, he gave credit where credit was due. He wrote:

Birmingham, Ala. Public Library Archives.

This is Fourth Avenue North between Nineteenth and Twentieth Streets. Wooster owned the two, two-story buildings in the middle of the photo. The Havarty Furniture building still stands and was home to Forbes Piano from 1912-1996.

"*Before closing this paper, justice demands that we should briefly allude to the heroic and self-sacrificing conduct, during this epidemic, of that unfortunate class who are known as "women of the town." These poor creatures, though outcasts from society, anathematized by the church, despised by women, and maltreated by men, when the pestilence swept over the city, came forth from their homes to nurse the sick and close the eyes of the dead. It was passing strange that they would receive no pay, expected no thanks; they only went where their presence was needed, and never remained longer than they could do good. While we abhor the degradation of these unfortunates, their magnanimous behavior during these fearful days has drawn forth our sympathy and gratitude.*"

Lou Wooster retired in 1901 and rented the buildings that housed her brothel to other more typical businesses. In 1908 she moved to a house on Birmingham's southside to live out her years.

She had become a wealthy woman and traveled throughout the United States and possibly Europe, Australia and Asia. But you can never be sure with Lou Wooster.

One thing has been consistent over the years in our fair state. When Alabama doesn't like the narrative, it reinvents or retells the story to reflect how they want to be perceived. Lou Wooster was no different. In 1911 she published a book about her life called *The Autobiography of a Magdalen*. Wooster was a wealthy woman, but she was not part of Birmingham society, and it probably pained her greatly. Her book was a way of rehabilitating her image and maybe reinventing her story. It also took some jabs at Birmingham's "good people." The people who would not

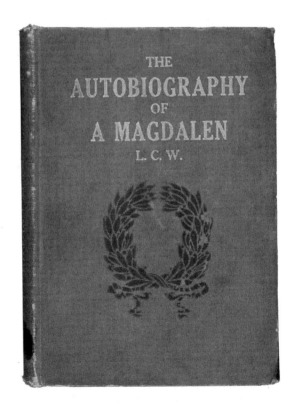

accept her socially but used her services regularly.

One story, in particular, stands out. During the early stages of the civil war, Wooster claims to have had a passionate romantic relationship with John Wilkes Booth. Booth was an actor and could have traveled to Montgomery, where they met and started their relationship. And since Booth was dead following the assassination of President Lincoln, he could not dispute the facts. Wooster claimed that Booth was still alive and would communicate with her from time to time. This story helped keep her name in national papers and in the hearts of those who considered Booth a hero.

Louise Wooster died on May 16, 1913. She was 71 years old. The funeral was held at her home, and she was buried at Oak Hill Cemetery. Rumor has it that gentleman from Birmingham who could not be seen attending her funeral sent their empty carriages in respect due to the propriety of the times. In reality, her funeral was sparsely attended.

Lou Wooster's image rehabilitation may not have gone as far as she hoped, but her name has lived on. A downtown loft was named after her, and an opera was written based on her book. Many people still believe that "Belle Watling" from *Gone with the Wind* was based on her.

Depending on where you get your information on Lou Wooster, it may be hard to know the truth. But the one thing that is true is that Birmingham might have ceased to exist if it wasn't for Lou and the others who stayed behind to take care of the sick and the dead in the summer of 1873. They truly saved the city.

Part 6

THE LAND

Alabama is one of the most biologically diverse
states in the country. It's the most diverse state east
of the Mississippi, with only large western states
with more diversity. We have a wide assortment of
plants, animals, waterways and minerals. It's our
land that makes us who we are in Alabama.
In this section, we feature unique town names,
a notorious plant and if you can't go over the
mountain, you move the mountain.

Birmingham's Cut In Red Mountain

Birmingham is located at the end of the Appalachian Mountain chain. Inevitably when you mention the words Red Mountain or Shades Mountain to someone who lives out west or even eastern Tennessee, they always have to compare their mountains with yours. Sure, they may not be as tall as the Rocky mountains, but anyone who has walked or biked over these hills will agree that they are mountains.

Red Mountain was one of the main reasons Birmingham is located where it is. The red ore mined from the mountain's slopes was one of the main ingredients for steel, all of which are located right around Jones Valley. For decades the mountain was dotted with entrances to mines with names such as Valley View, Lone Pine, and Spaulding mines. The mines were all slope mines, with most openings facing north towards Birmingham and sloping south along the iron ore seam.

Despite all the mining taking place on the moun-

Courtesy of the Library of Congress, Prints and Photographs Division

"The Cut" looking north from Homewood towards Birmingham.

tain, crossing the mountain from Birmingham to Shades Valley was no easy feat in the early 20th century. There are natural gaps in any mountain range that people have exploited to cross over. We take for granted today the gaps that are still there. For Birmingham locals, here are a few you may recognize.

- Irondale Gap is at the top of Pawnee Avenue before it becomes Montclair Road.
- If you travel Arlington Avenue South up the mountain and past the roundabout into English Village, that is Brown's Gap.
- Where Richard Arrington Boulevard crosses the mountain below Vulcan is Lone Pine Gap.
- Further down where Green Springs crosses the mountain is Walker's Gap
- Graces Gap is where Spaulding-Ishkooda Road connects with West Valley Avenue and West Oxmoor Road in Homewood.

There are many other gaps to the east and west, but this will help with our story.

As more and more people were trying to leave the smoke and noise from the blast furnaces located around Birmingham, they looked south to the quiet and potential of Shades Valley. The most direct way to get there was Lone Pine Gap.

At the top, you would cross the mineral railroad, which carried ore across the slope of red mountain, moving from the southside to the northside at lone pine gap and then back again at graces gap. Lone Pine Gap was also known as the "pig trail." This nickname would be celebrated years later with the opening of the Pig Trail Inn in downtown Homewood. A popular hangout for local teens.

Sometimes when you want real change, it takes a developer. Troupe Brazleton and Stephen Smith were developing the Edgewood Lake resort and Edgewood residential subdivision in what would become the town of Homewood. They needed a way to move people from Birmingham efficiently, so they created the Edgewood Electric Railway. In 1909 they struck a deal to lower the roadbed at Lone Pine Gap by about 50 feet or so, passing under the Mineral Railroad. Jefferson County contributed to the project in return for establishing a 16-foot-wide right of way for automobile traffic, turning the "pig trail" into a proper route of transportation into the valley.

This route through Lone Pine Gap would eventually become Alabama State Highway 31, also known as Montgomery Highway. Highway 31 starts in Spanish Fort, Alabama, close to Mobile, and travels to Tennessee. For many years it was a primary source of traffic through Jefferson County.

In the 1950s, construction on interstate 65 started. This major highway would closely parallel Highway 31 in Alabama. The route chosen to cross Red Mountain was at Walker's Gap, where Green Springs Highway crossed to the west of the city of Birmingham.

The suburbs south of the city were quickly growing. Homewood, Mountain Brook, and Vestavia were adding to their population, and a lot of those people were traveling down Highway 280 and Highway 31 and crossing at Lone Pine

Looking north from the cut towards the Highland Avenue bridge. Highland Plaza is on the left and Highland Towers is on the right.

Gap, which had not changed much in the previous decades. Travelers needed another route over the mountain, and discussions started.

As early as 1908, there had been discussions about building a tunnel through Red Mountain. By the 1920s, local architect George Turner had created renderings of what the tunnel would look like. In 1946, New York Tunnel expert Ole Singstad was brought to the city to survey proposed tunnel locations. He favored a tunnel from 22nd Street South in Birmingham to 21st Avenue in Homewood.

If you don't know the name Ole Singstad, you may know some of his projects. Singstad designed the Lincoln Tunnel, the Brooklyn–Battery Tunnel, and the Queens–Midtown Tunnel in New York, to name just a few.

The idea of constructing a tunnel was passed around for the next decade. In 1959 the Birmingham City Commission declined to fund a study further, agreeing not to "spend Birmingham taxpayers' money to give Mountain Brook travelers convenience."

It looked like there would be no tunnel, but the problem still existed. If there was no money and no enthusiasm to drill through the mountain, what if they could move the mountain? A new report was commissioned and presented in 1960 to the downtown improvement association and Jefferson County Commission with ideas.

Engineers evaluated 23 possible routes, which were narrowed to six preferred routes. Even though the tunnel was left for dead, three options were tunnels. All options started at 26th Street South in Birmingham.

Not to jump ahead in our story, but I bet you have never noticed that there is no 26th Street South, north of University Boulevard.

Birmingham News columnist Walling Keith said the real question about that proposed Red Mountain expressway is not whether we should have it, but rather, how soon can we get it? He wrote, "we really ought to get that Red Mountain Expressway cut before we shoot a man to the moon!"

The option chosen, "cut route D," had the least cost when purchasing right of ways and moving dirt. A large portion of Homewoods African-American community, Rosedale, was bulldozed for the southern entrance to the expressway and Rosedale Drive.

Not as many homes were demolished on the northern side of the mountain. About a half dozen houses had been slated for demolition. The homes on the crest and north side were more stately than in Rosedale, and some owners would not move without a fight. There were legal fights over losing a family home, and when that was lost, disputes continued over how much the home and property were worth. Negotiations continued through 1965 on property values.

Next in line for the bulldozer was historic Highland Avenue and the Highland Towers and Highland Plaza apartments, which were dead ahead. Instead of going through the properties, the expressway would plunge underneath Highland Avenue before reappearing on the other side. Residents were not convinced that this project would be successful, which would come within feet of their apartments. They worried about the noise and the dust, and they were not convinced their apartment homes would not be damaged.

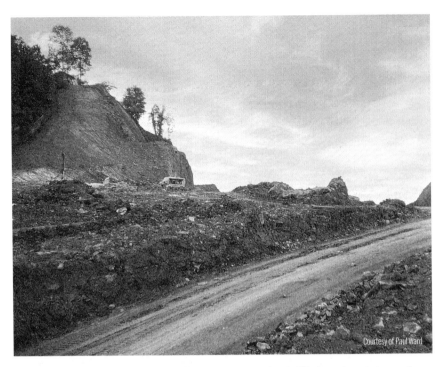

Looking south from the north slope of the mountain. The final roadbead will be lower than what we see here.

Harbert Construction Company handled the project, and John Harbert himself mounted a PR campaign to sell the project to a skeptical public. Harbert hosted cocktail parties for apartment residents to explain the process. He set up bleachers so people could view the machinery moving the earth around. He gave out balloons and ice cream. The "good neighbor" PR campaign was a huge success and went a long way in soothing rattled nerves from the dynamiting of the mountain and the street closings and traffic created by the project.

In what usually would have taken three months, Harbert completed the Highland Avenue part of the project in record time. Using every available machine from jobs around the southeast, they dug around the clock and completed this part of the project in less than two weeks.

Digging and grading took seven years, from 1962 until 1969, and the Red Mountain Expressway was opened to traffic in 1970. Workers removed 2 million cubic yards from the ridge of Red Mountain.

When the roads were widened at Lone Pine Gap and Walkers Gap, the iron ore seam was exposed for travelers to view. Industrialist Erskine Ramsey donated metal signs that said, "This Red Mountain iron ore is the basis of Birmingham's Iron-Steel Industry." There were two tags mounted on the top and the bottom of the seam. You can see them today, but you may have to look close due to vegetation growing out of the rock.

The Red Mountain cut exposed the iron ore seam and over 190 million years of geologic strata dating to over 500 million years ago. The Ordovician, Silurian, Devonian, and Mississippian geologic periods are visible in the cut. Special features include caves, volcanic ash layers, the Red Mountain fault line, prehistoric reefs and beaches, fossils, and fossil tracks.

UAB geologists were excited to see the newly exposed strata late in the construction. They were also appalled that the exposed rock would be covered with spray concrete. One scientist took it upon himself to stop it by laying down in front of the concrete spray truck. An emergency appeal to the governor stopped the spraying and left the rock exposed. But not all of it. There are a few slopes that are covered to this day.

The cut exposed roughly as much geological data as can be found in the Grand Canyon in the space of just eighteen hundred and fifty linear feet. Scientists from as far away as France came to study the exposed cut.

And when you have something that impressive, you need a museum to show it off. The Lin-Henley Charitable Trust pledged $250,000 to create the Red Mountain Museum on the slope of the mountain. There was even a paved trail that extended along one of the tiers of the cut.

The Red Mountain Museum eventually merged with the Discovery Place Museum. They moved to the former Loveman's building in downtown Birmingham and is now known as the McWane Center.

The road was dedicated as the Elton B. Stephens Expressway in honor of local businessman and philanthropist Elton B. Stephens, who chaired the Birmingham and Jefferson County Freeway and Expressway Committee. Those of us in Birmingham call it the Red Mountain Expressway.

For years, Highway 31 took a left turn just past the Oxmoor Road/Hollywood Boulevard intersection into downtown Homewood. With the cut in the mountain, travelers would go straight and then travel what seems to be halfway up the mountain to where the cut started. You may not notice it, but the road through the mountain makes an "S" curve to make it more visually appealing.

After leaving the mountain, the elevated expressway continued north to an abrupt halt within sight of Interstate 20/59. Travelers would have to exit the expressway at first avenue north or second avenue north. Directly ahead was a new postal facility, and the year before, the famed Terminal Station was demolished for a proposed Social Security Administration Building. It seems the expressway had nowhere to go.

The rumor was that Governor George Wallace would not help fund the project as punishment for Birmingham residents not supporting him in earlier campaigns for governor. Of course, this could not have been possible since he was not in office at the time. It does make for a good story.

With the continued population growth south of the city of Birmingham, the Red Mountain Expressway has been a vital link to the city of Birmingham and areas north. And in the end, it makes for a very convenient trip for Mountain Brook travelers.

◢ THE LAND

Where did that town name come from?

When I was researching my book on Shades Cahaba High School, I learned about areas right around me in Jefferson County that had different names a century ago. Hedona was named after the Hedona Mine on Red Mountain. After the mine shut down, the city of Mountain Brook rebranded the area as English Village. The town of Waddell became Mountain Brook Village. A little farther south was the town of Merkel. The flooding was so bad that they packed up and moved half a mile and became New Merkel. It is now called Cahaba Heights. Even farther south by the Cahaba river was Mud Town, an old Indian trading post.

ALABAMA

If I am honest, I am probably more than a little jealous of these names; you see, my hometown, Homewood, has a boring name. It just doesn't have the same panache as Scratch Ankle or Majestic.

Alabama has its fair share of interesting town

Buzzard Roost Covered Bridge in Colbert County, Alabama, three miles west of Cherokee.

names. Of course, we would. A lot of cultures have passed through our state. The French, Spanish, and English all have left their mark. So did the different Indian nations. They left names we use today, some with our own Alabama pronunciations. There are other names chosen due to laziness or maybe due to being under the influence of local mash. Not really; they just seem that way. Some of the towns I will introduce you to may no longer be around.

I want to start it off with one of my favorite town names, Arab. It reminds me of a joke.

A southerner and a Yankee were in a car driving. The Yankee said, "where are we going?" "Arab," said the southerner. "How do you spell it?" said the Yankee. "A-R-A-B," replied the southerner. "You idiot," laughed the Yankee, "that spells Arab as in someone from the middle east!" The two friends argued back and forth all the way there. The southerner said, "I'll show you." And he pulled into a parking lot. A lanky man came around to the driver's window. The southerner said, "would you tell my friend where were we are!" The lanky man slowly walked around the front of the car to the passenger's window. He leaned down, stuck his head in the window, and said, "you are at the Dairy Queen."

That kills with my friends from Arab.

The name was supposed to be Arad with a d. Named after the postmaster's son, the federal officials misspelled what was on the application. Dairy Queen would be an excellent name for a town, though.

Speaking of the government, one postmaster kept sending in names for a new town only to get rejected repeatedly. He decided to give it one more chance, and Chance, Alabama, was born.

INDIAN NAMES

There are way more towns in Alabama with Indian names or anglicized versions of an Indian name than I can possibly talk about in a short story. Here is a greatest hits list, and let's start with our state name, Alabama. It came from a Choctaw phrase that means either "thicket-clearers" or "plant cutters."

You may know Sylacauga as "Marble City," famous for its white marble. But, the name is a derivative of the Indian word 'chalakage,' which means "The Place of the Chalaka Tribe."

The following words are from the Muskogee or Creek language.

- Loachapoka comes from 'loca poga' or where the turtles live/sit.
- Notasulga is from 'noti sulgi' or many teeth.
- Opelika is from 'opilwa lako' or big swamp.
- Wetumpka is from 'wewau tumcau' or rumbling water.
- Wedowee comes from a Creek Indian chief whose town was close to a stream by the same name. It means "old water."

And my favorite is Eastaboga. It is named for an upper creek village, Istpoka, which means "Where the people reside." It's my favorite place because when I was younger, I would use the phrase "from here to Eastaboga," which meant a long

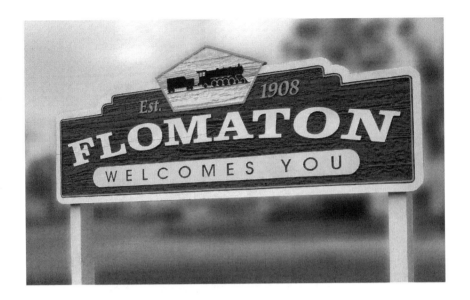

way. "We can't go there! It's all the way to Eastaboga!" I thought it was a made-up name until we were driving east on I-20, and I saw the Eastaboga exit.

COMBINED NAMES

When deciding on a name for your new town, you can use one of the millions of names available to you worldwide, or you can make up a new name. These three Alabama towns decided to create their own.

Flomaton, in Escambia County and right on the Florida state line, took the "Flo" from Florida, the "ma" from Alabama, "ton" for town, and created a town name that flows off the tongue.

In Covington County and directly east of Flomaton, Florala took the "Flor" from Florida, "ala" from Alabama to come up with their unique town name.

In Marion County, there is Guin, and a mere 6 miles away is Winfield. When coming up with a name for a new town between these two towns, they took the first syllables of the town's name they are located between and created Gu-Win. It's not confusing at all.

COMPANY TOWN

Some towns would not exist if not for the company located there, bringing work to the area. Some towns popped up around an existing general store. Here are a few:

Blues Old Stand in Bullock County is named for Mr. Blue's nineteenth-century general store, or "stand," as he called it.

Brilliant in Marion County is not named for the intelligence of its people or because it was an excellent place for a town. It was named for the Brilliant Coal Company.

The Alabama Fruit Growers and Winery Association wanted to create a center for grape-growing and winemaking in Cleburne County. They chose an area around a town called Zidonia. The company recruited mainly northern Europeans, Swedes, Danes, and Norwegians, and the town grew rapidly. The citizens held a contest to rename the town, and they chose Fruithurst, with "hurst" meaning "grove" in German.

Photo courtesy of Jimmy Emerson, DVM

Phenix City in Russell County is located on the west side of the Chattahoochee River. The original name was Lively, and it was changed in 1897. The change was probably for Phenix Mills, the major employer across the river in Columbus, Georgia.

MOONSHINE MOTIVATED

Moonshine has been big business in Alabama because of prohibition in the 1920s and early 30s. And for Alabama's insistence on dry counties after the ban was lifted. So, of course, moonshine would make an appearance in town names.

Take, for instance, Scant City. This town in Marshall County was called that because the moonshiners sold their product in 12-ounce bottles known as "scant pints."

The town of Frog Eye in Tallapoosa County got its name back during prohibition. There was a saloon in the community that sold illegal liquor. There was a frog in the window, and if one eye was closed, they could not safely sell the liquor. A lawman might have been inside at the time. Both eyes open meant it was safe to buy.

If you lived in the notoriously dry north Alabama and didn't want to visit the moonshiners, you would need to take a quick trip to Tennessee for your liquor. Zip City in Lauderdale County got its name because of all the cars zipping through the town to buy in Tennessee. The town was immortalized by the band Drive-By Truckers, who featured a song called "Zip City" on their 2001 album "Southern Rock Opera."

QUESTIONABLE NAMES

There are innocent town names at first glance, but 13-year old Shawn cannot see them as anything but naughty. I want to keep this book accessible for everyone, so I will keep those to myself. I will tell you about Boar Tush in Winston County, established in 1885. It was also known as Boar Tusk. I guess the postmaster wanted to make sure he covered both ends of the pig.

ANIMALS

Keeping with our animal theme, Scratch Ankle was named because of the abundance of cows in the area. I believe the cows roamed freely, and the cows brought fleas to the people, and the fleas made everyone scratch their ankles.

Chigger Hill was named when the original settlers had to fight off a mite infestation. Why would you stay if there was a mite infestation? Many towns moved to get out of the floods or be closer to new rail lines. I think a mite infestation is a great reason to move.

Flea Hop got its name from fleas that would jump on people from local goats. They changed their name to Santuck, which incidentally has a Flea Market.

And Bug Tussle has two origination stories. The first is that someone climbed a mountain and said all the tiny people below looked like bugs tussling. What were those people doing to make him think that? The second, and more believable to me, was a man named Charlie Campbell, who loved to drink the local mash. One day he was deep into a bottle when he noticed two bugs rolling a ball of dirt across the road. He said the bugs appeared to be tussling.

MILEAGE

Some towns couldn't be bothered with a name, and they just wanted you to know how far they were from somewhere else.

Fourmile is located four miles from Columbiana. There is a Six Mile in Morgan County and one in Bibb county. I can't figure out what would be six miles to either of those locations. They are possibly named after a six-mile-long creek. And Eight Mile is located eight miles from Mobile.

Center Point in Jefferson County is named because it is the halfway point between the road to Chalkville and the one to Pinson. At least, that is what I have been told. It seems a little out of the way.

Centre is in the middle of Cherokee County, and Midway in Bullock County is located between two towns.

Photo courtesy of Jimmy Emerson, DVM

WHAT DID THEY SAY?

Some towns are named after a phrase that someone said. These are some of my favorites, and they show a sense of humor in the people in those towns.

Needmore in Pike County came from a resident who thought the community "needed more of everything." It was a name upgrade from Rough Log.

When an unavailable item was asked for at a general store in Elmore County in the 1920s, the owner would say, "I'm Slap Out." The town of Slapout found its name.

When the law raided a cockfight in Henry County, someone yelled, "Grab all the money and run!" They decided Graball would be an excellent name for a town.

Ino in Coffee County was chosen from suggestions. When the postmaster asked for a name, everybody spoke at once. One person kept saying, "I know. I know. I know."

With little time on their hands, farmers at a Covington County store would "load and go." Loango was an appropriate name for this town.

PINES

You can't take a walk in Alabama without running into a pine tree. In fact, the timber industry has been a vital part of our state's economy for a long time. Of course, with all the trees and industry, we would have the word pine in a few town names. I have counted at least 19 of them. They include Pine Branch, Pine Dale, Pine Grove, Pine Hill, Pine Level, Pine Tucky, and the list goes on. My favorite would be Pine Apple, where my grandmother grew up. It's not a pineapple like the tropical fruit but Pine and Apple. I guess two trees are better than one.

DODGED A BULLET

Not every town starts with a great name or even a funny name. These towns had questionable names but made the switch.

The town of Oxford in Calhoun County had the good sense to change its name from Lickskillet. Supposedly it was named because the townspeople were so poor that they had to lick their skillets to obtain enough food to survive.

Greenville in Butler County also made the smart choice of naming their town after Greenville, South Carolina, where many early residents had moved from. The original name was Buttsville, named after Samual Butts, who died fighting Creek Indians. The name change saved townspeople the indignity of becoming the butt of the joke.

Jugtown is just north of Birmingham, named after a local jug factory. Someone called the area the "garden spot of the state," and wiser heads prevailed, renaming the town Gardendale, much to the delight of my wife and her family.

Gardendale, the "garden spot of the state," should not be confused with Garden City just up the road in Cullman County, which proclaims to be the "garden center of the world."

Dauphin Island was called Massacre Island by the French after Iberville found sixty headless skeletons there. Good thing they renamed it Dauphin, which is

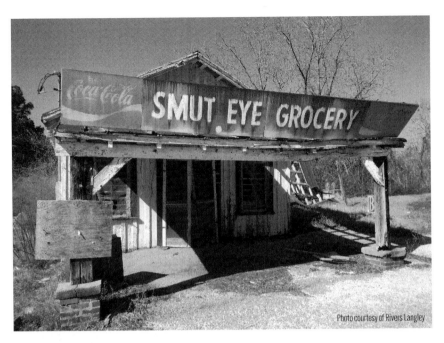

Photo courtesy of Rivers Langley

Smut Eye Grocery in Smuteye, Alabama.

a French prince, the heir to the throne. Can you imagine selling your family on going to Massacre Island for spring break?

MISCELLANEOUS

Here are some additional towns worthy of pointing out:

I always thought Eclectic was an interesting name for a town. Eclectic is defined as having a "broad and diverse range." An example would be he has an eclectic taste in music. The town was founded by Dr. M. L. Fielder, a practitioner of eclectic medicine. He thought that the word meant "best."

The mining industry in Alabama created towns and certainly influenced town names. The town of Slick Lizard got its name from local miners who had to crawl on their bellies through clay portals about 2 feet high and would come out "slick as a lizard."

And we can't do a story about Alabama towns without mentioning Smut Eye. In fact, there have been two Smut Eyes in Alabama. A certain blacksmith's shop in Bullock County served a drink the local women called the devil's brew. As the men stood around the fire, drinking and talking, their faces would get smudged except for their eyes. It was a dead giveaway, and the women started calling the shop and then the community Smut Eye.

In Coffee County, there was a Smut Eye that has been renamed Victoria. It has a similar story where local men would stand around a fire outside of the general store and become covered in soot.

I could go on and on, but I need to wind this story down somewhere. There are great names and interesting origination stories for towns across our state that I could write a book. And someone has. You can start with *Place Names in Alabama* by Virginia Foscue.

I will leave you with some final town names I like.

Frog Level (there are three)	Dog Town
Tallasee	Gobblers Crossing
Froggy Bottom	Dismal
Possum Trot	Carbon Hill
Possum Bend	Burnt Corn
Ceasarville	Axis
Suspension	Allgood
Postoak	Needmore
Ox Level	Old Texas
Excel	Phil Campbell
Fisanor	Rash
Listerhill	Robjohn
Duck Springs	Shinbone Valley
Echo	Screamer

Toadvine

Vinegar Bend

Trickem

Sunny South

Dolomite

Hackleburg

Bacon Level

Coffee Pot

Burn Out

Intercourse

Normal

Sunflower

Sunny South

Blow Gourd

Lizard Lope

Deer Head

Murder Creek

Mud Tavern

Pea Ridge

Pig eye

Rehobeth

Spit Box

Yampertown

Weogufka

Vinegar Bend

Coal Fire

Five Forks

Climax

Seman

Shorter

Gamble

Scarce Grease

Cattail Pond

Kudzu

I worked at Mr. Gatti's Pizza when I was in high school. One of my co-workers was an on and off again theatre major. He had big dreams, as all creatives do. He wanted to be an actor and make movies. He told me about a movie idea he had, called "Kudzilla." The story is about an innocuous weed from Japan. It comes to our shores and turns into a monster that attacks the American South. Imagine an actor in a kudzu costume destroying cardboard buildings much like Godzilla did when he first appeared in the 1954 Japanese movie of the same name.

I always thought this was an excellent idea for a film, and I tucked it away in my mind as a future project. My co-worker must not have done anything with it. At least I have never seen or heard of it. It's probably a little too close to reality to make into a film. We don't have to imagine kudzu destroying or even just covering buildings. It's happening here in the south. Just at a

ALABAMA

Scouts from Troop 97 in Homewood, hiking on an existing trail through Kudzu at Red Mountain Park.

much slower rate than a movie would allow. But is it really as bad as we think?

While kudzu is not uniquely Alabama, you can see it all over the state. So much that I thought it would make for a good short story.

One of my favorite kudzu patches is at Red Mountain Park in Birmingham. On the west end of the park, there is a large open area around the #10 mine. You will find oversized chairs funded and built by scouts for their Eagle projects that ring this area. The sides of the hills and ravine are covered in kudzu. The best view is looking up into the site from the Redding Trail. The trail is a road, and during peak growing season, vines from the patch are trying to work their way across the road, only to be beaten back by maintenance workers and the inevitable freeze that will come in winter.

From this open area, you can duck back into the woods and continue to hike down one of the many trails. Do you know what is not in these woods? Kudzu.

I will explain that, but first a little history lesson. Kudzu is not unique to Alabama. You can find it everywhere in the south. It was first introduced to the Unit-

Kudzu on a hillside above the #10 Mine at Red Mountain Park.

ed States during the Philadelphia Centennial Exposition in 1876. It was touted as a great ornamental plant for its sweet-smelling blooms and sturdy vines.

But it was a man from Georgia who got behind the plant and promoted it strongly. Channing Cope worked for the Atlanta Journal Consitution, where he wrote a gardening column. He also had a popular radio show, and it was his opinion that the true wealth of the south was in our soil. The south was mainly an agrarian society then, and he preached that erosion was a problem and would only get worse. This was before the dust bowls of the 1930s, when severe droughts and a failure to apply dry farming techniques led to wind erosion in the west.

Cope's idea was a system where you rotated cattle grazing on kudzu and natural grass. Kudzu grows like crazy, and the cows could efficiently fight back the spread by eating it.

If you are a farmer that wants to feed your cattle the nutritious kudzu, you have a few problems. First off, it takes a few years for kudzu to establish. Second, your cattle will eat it faster than you can get it established. And finally, you can't bale it.

Kudzu on Red Mountain just below The Club and above the Vulcan Trail.

The vines would gum a bailing machine during the first few minutes you started bailing it.

The Army Corps of Engineers decided kudzu was all that was needed for erosion control. They ignored the other options this nutritious, edible, medicinal, and useful fiber could bring us. They also didn't consider that the weed would get out of control.

Here's a funny thing. Kudzu is not as prevalent as you may think. In one report I read, kudzu only covers about 250,000 acres. In comparison, privet, another invasive species, covers 3.2 million acres. Kudzus is not as pervasive as we think it is, and there are a couple of reasons for this. One is that we mistake kudzu for other similar-looking vines such as tropical creepers and cat's claw creeper.

I watched a presentation on Kudzu by Alabama naturalist Bill Finch, and he mentioned why we think kudzu is more persuasive than it really is.

Vines only grow in a place called galleries. These would be streams and other open areas where light makes it to the forest floor. As humans came in and created more trails and roads, we created more galleries. We had to dig out and level the landscape when we created paved roads making long and wide galleries. And following the Army Corps of Engineers' advice, we used kudzu to limit erosion. And since we don't let the cows out of the pasture to graze along our roads, kudzu continues to grow.

Remember when I told you that at Red Mountain Park, I would leave the area with all the kudzu for the forest, and there would be no more kudzu? The same thing is happening along the roadway. If you see a lot of kudzu along the road, and you park your car and walk in the woods, you would not see kudzu. But we tend to think that the kudzu just keeps going and going.

Godzilla always had an enemy to battle. In my version of "Kudzilla," our enemy is pretty docile. I send out a herd of hungry cows who, in a couple of days' time, consume Kudzilla. It doesn't make for riveting viewing, but our hero is the cow.

In the podcast episode of this story, The Alabama Short Stories Players performed for the first and only time, my radio play *"Gone with the Kudzilla."* I have included the script for you here. I just ask that you read it in really bad southern accents.

GONE WTH THE KUDZILLA

Robert bursts into the room: *Elizabeth, I have some terrible news.*

Elizabeth: *What is it, Robert?*

Robert: *The great Japanese monster Kudzilla has landed on our shores and is headed straight for this house.*

Elizabeth: *Oh no! What are we going to do?*

Robert: *We will have to take decisive action to see that our way of life is upheld.*

Elizabeth: *When did you first hear about Kudzilla?*

Robert: *I have known about it all my life.*

Elizabeth: *Really? And only now its become a threat?*

Robert: *It's always been a threat, a slow creeping threat. I have watched it take over abandoned buildings all across our state.*

Elizabeth: *When did Kudzilla land on our shores?*

Robert: *1876*

Elizabeth: *1876?? That's almost 150 years ago, and now it's a threat?*

Robert: *It's a slow, creeping, menacing threat.*

Elizabeth: *Ok, ok, it's a threat, but what will we do about it? What about the children?*

Robert: *I have called in reinforcements. Colonel Blackburn has agreed to bring in his troops.*

Elizabeth: *Are you talking about old man Blackburn from the farm down the road? Is he a colonel?*

Robert: *Not exactly, but he has cows, hungry cows, and he has agreed to move them to our field to fight Kudzilla. Within a few days, the cows will consume every leaf and vine in that field, sending Kudzilla back to the sea from which it came.*

Elizabeth: *That far?*

Robert: *Well, more like our property line, but you get the idea.*

Elizabeth: *As God as my witness, those cows will never be hungry again!*

Colonel Blackburn: *Mr. Robert, Miss Elizabeth! We have fought back Kudzilla but have discovered an even stronger enemy!*

Robert: *Who?*

Colonel Blackburn: *Privet*

Robert: *I'll think about the privet tomorrow.*

Elizabeth: *After all, tomorrow is another day.*

THE END

Part 7

THE ARTISTS

There are people creating art all over this state and they have been creating it long before it was ever a state. There are diverse groups of painters, sculptors, photographers and more working for profit and some, just for the love of their art. I have always had a special place in my heart for artists. My father, brother and myself are all graphic designers and we all have this desire to create something. The four people featured in this section are all as diverse as the mediums they chose to work with.

She Paints On Spider Webs

I was an art major in college and have a Bachelor of Fine Arts to prove it. My goal was to be a graphic designer, but to earn that hallowed degree, I created a lot of fine art along the way. Wood sculpting, stone carving, oil painting, and acrylic painting, to name a few. Some mediums are more difficult than others.

When he heard about my Alabama Short Stories podcast, my father, himself an art major, suggested I look into the story of the woman who painted on spider webs. What? How does one paint on spider webs?

Luckily, the master of the spider web painting me-

dium spent most of her life in Huntsville, Alabama.

Anne Clopton was born in 1878 in Fayette-ville, Tennessee. In 1896 she moved with her family to Huntsville, Alabama. Her father, Professor R.S. Bradshaw, was to become president of the Huntsville Female Seminary. One of the first girl's schools in Alabama.

Anne Clopton viewing one of her spider web canvases

As a child, Anne took drawing classes, and she showed talent. When she was 11 years old, a teacher gave her art magazines to help foster that talent. In one of those, she read an article about a German artist who painted on spider webs. Painting on webs intrigued her, so she spent years trying and failing to paint on spider webs, eventually mastering this unique technique. The article never mentioned how the artist was able to do this, so she had to figure it out herself. She even gave up playing with other children for a while while she perfected this skill.

Spider web painting is not new. Monks and peasant artists in the 16th century would gather cobwebs from spiders and caterpillars. They would build up layers of silk to be the foundation of portraits and landscapes. This technique was unique to artists in the Tyrolean Alps in Western Austria and Northern Italy. These paintings were small, and there are less than 100 known in existence today.

It was only years later that Anne found out that the German artist she was trying to copy was painting on thick layers of cobwebs, which would have made things much easier for her. Through persistence and by accident, Clopton became the only artist who could paint on individual spider webs.

Anne initially searched for spider webs around her home. She tried ones from shrubs around the house, but they were too thin and fragile. Anne would go to the attic of her home or the loft of a neighbor's barn for webs. They were usually coated with dust and so weak they would collapse before she could get them home. The only web she found she could paint on was of the common grass spider.

Once she found her "canvas," she then had to find the right paint. Watercolor paints wouldn't work because the paint would crack when it dried. Oil paints worked best because they took longer to dry, and it still had some flexibility that seemed to work on the web canvas.

Once she perfected her process, Anne would collect webs in August and September, which is when she found they were the strongest. She would make small frames out of cardboard. Anne would then take them to the web, place the frame underneath, and gently capture the web, which would stick to the frame naturally. She would then take a second, identical frame and sandwich the web so it would stay in place. She could then store them and let them dry until she was ready to paint.

There was a time limit on when she could use her webs. She would collect them in summer to paint on in winter. If she waited any longer, the webs would become too dry and brittle to paint on.

Early in her career as a cobweb painter, she became somewhat of a joke around town. Not a day went by that she did not receive word from a housewife saying that her house had some first-class cobwebs and she should run right over with a cardboard square and remove them. They figured if she just found a man, she would get over this silly hobby.

The jokes and comments hurt, but Anne continued to work on her art.

Clopton's painting of Big Spring in Huntsville. You can just see the spider web in the sky which was stretched and dried in the frame.

Painting was her favorite part of the process, but she loved the hunt. She knew the habits of the spiders, and she would go in search of the perfect web. Eventually, her neighbors came around to her art, and they would keep on the lookout for perfect webs and would alert her when they found one.

Painting on the delicate webs needed a special touch. Anne would dab paint using a technique called stippling or pointillism. You would recognize this technique in the works of impressionist painter Georges Seurat. Trust me; you know his work.

She found that applying the paint with a stroke would break the delicate web. She also found that she needed to thin the oil paint to make it flow, and turpentine worked best. Small portions would be painted and then allowed to dry. When the painting was finished, she would frame it behind glass to protect the finished piece.

Painting on cobwebs was a time-consuming process. A small image may take a month of constant work, while the largest would be about 8"x10" in size and could take as long as three months to complete.

When she finally figured out the best way to apply paint, she started work on her first piece. She noticed that the weight of the paint was making the web sag, so she decided to end her work for the day and come back the next. The following morning she was shocked to find that the spider had come back and repaired the damage by spinning a new web over her work. After spending a couple of hours fixing what the spider had done, her mother called her to dinner, and she stopped for the day.

Imagine her surprise that on the third day, she found that the spider had again, fixed the web. It was then that Anne realized she would have to find a way to remove the web from its original location and away from the spider.

This story may be the first time you have heard of this artist, and if you live in Huntsville, you may be surprised to hear it happened in your town. But back in the day, she was well known. She had been featured in magazine articles and on radio programs. There are even two pictures on permanent display at the Smithsonian Institution in Washington, D.C.

In 1938 she came to the attention of Dave Elman, host of the nationally broadcasted *Hobby Lobby* show. Not to be confused with the craft store today. He invited her to his show that was broadcast from Studio 8 at Rockefeller Center on the NBC network.

That next year she appeared with Elman again at his Hobby Lobby House at the 1939 Worlds Fair in New York City to exhibit her paintings. She was also featured in the newsreel *Industry on Parade*, which celebrated her art business as an example of American Free enterprise.

In 1940 Universal Picture Corporation sent a representative to her home to make a motion picture of her painting process and story. It became part of Universal's *Stranger than Fiction* newsreel. It was shown worldwide to soldiers in hospitals and camps during World War 2.

Dave Elman became a big fan because, in 1943, she was invited back to New

York, this time to appear on his show that moved to the CBS network.

Dave Elman was a big deal. So much so that When Elman went on vacation on August 2, 1939, First Lady Eleanor Roosevelt accepted the invitation to be his replacement as host. The two would collaborate on shows for soldiers during the war.

Even still, Anne had plenty to do that didn't involve spiders. In 1926, Anne, her husband, and her growing family moved into a house on Triana Boulevard. She took a cedar-lined closet that was just large enough for a small table and chair to be her art studio.

She raised five children and taught at Huntsville's Joe Bradley High School for 32-years, retiring in 1944. She also organized and led the first Girl Scout Troop in Huntsville for 15 years. And to add one more hobby to the list, she bred Persian cats. Having cats and painting on cobwebs seems like a recipe for disaster.

After her time in the classroom, Anne Clopton ran for the Madison County board of education, the first woman to do so, but was defeated by the incumbent.

It is thought that Anne created more than 700 paintings over the years, most of which have been lost. Many are in the collections of private owners. Who knows how many of those are still around due to accidents or general deterioration. A lot of the paintings were destroyed at the Worlds Fair. People would poke holes in them to see if they were real.

The technique Anne devised to paint on a single web is what ultimately will lead to her work disappearing. The German artists of the 16th century built up thick layers of webs for their work, which will help them survive much longer.

Anne Clopton died on February 4, 1956, leaving behind her husband, James Clopton, two sons, three daughters, 11 grandchildren, and one great-grandchild.

Today, Anne Clopton's home is a local business called Dream Makers, a new age metaphysical gift shop and alternative health center. When owners Ron and Jerrine Gray found out about the home's history, they went about recreating Anne's closet studio and helping to preserve her history. They recreated the closet based on photos. When they moved into the house, they found brushes, paints, and other art supplies in the house that are used in the display. And now it's a small museum celebrating the life and work of Anne Clopton.

Painting on cobwebs is an art that has died out. But maybe one day, another child will read about Anne Clopton's painting on a cobweb and will want to try to do it themselves. Anne's art legacy is that she left her art and her techniques behind as a starting point.

Clopton having her work and process photographed in her studio.

The Portraits of William Frye

F amily portraits are kind of weird, don't you think? These old pictures that have been looking over the family for years. Some children feel like the eyes follow them around the room. Maybe they do. Portraits seemed weird to me as a kid. The older I got, the more interesting they became.

My parents have a set of portraits hanging in their living room of Ephraim H. Foster and his wife Susan A. Watkins. My third great-grandparents. They were married in 1847 in Lawrence County, Alabama. Probably Courtland, where they raised a family before moving to Decatur at the turn of the century.

These portraits were passed down in the family to their daughter Bettie Foster. To her daughter, Susie Pointer, then to my grandmother Elizabeth Malone and finally to my father. These portraits have hung for years over these mantels, and the more I have learned about the subjects, the more comforting they have become.

I guess you could say they were instrumental in me learning more about my family history.

Portraits have always been more than a record. They have also been used to show power, wealth, social standing, or some other qualities of the sitter. It is also all we had before the invention of the camera. A medium that would eventually let everyone, no matter their class or wealth, keep a record of who they were.

Collection of Leo Wright

Ephraim H. Foster

Portrait artists were not just in our nation's capitals and largest cities; they were all over, even in the Antebellum South.

One of those artists was G. Wilhelm Frye. The G was for George, but he never used that name. Frye is spelled F-R-Y-E. When he came to America, it was spelled F-R-E-Y, but he had trouble getting his mail, so according to his daughter, he changed it. His new, anglicized name is William Frye.

William Frye was born in Breslau, Prussia, on September 13, 1822, and raised in Vienna, Austria. He was educated at Heidelberg University and studied art in Prague, Bohemia. While there, he and two other students became fascinated with James Fenimore Cooper's stories of frontier and Native American life. They made plans to have an adventure in America. It was during the Christmas holidays when they were flush with cash that they made their plans. They made it as far as

Collection of Leo Wright

Susan W. Foster

the port of Bremen when the other two students backed out.

The allure of those landscapes called Frye, so he set sail without his friends, and after three months, in 1841, he landed in New York City and spent the next couple of years there. Luckily for Frye, his cousin Count Johann Schmidt was German Consul to New York, and I am sure that made his transition much more comfortable.

Frye was given letters to influential people throughout the country before he started working his way west. He moved to Kentucky for a few years before moving to Huntsville, Alabama. There he met the love of his life, Virginia Catherine Hale. The adventure that started in college, emigrating to America, visiting the West, and painting the landscapes ended here. They married on May 18, 1848, and would have four children.

He became a naturalized citizen in 1852 and called Huntsville home for the rest of his life.

Even though he lived in Huntsville, he had to travel throughout Alabama and the surrounding states to paint portraits of prominent families to make a living. He was setting up studios for a time in towns such as Selma, Greensboro, Natchez, and Jackson.

Courtesy of HMCPL Special Collections

"Big Spring at Huntsville" by William Frye

In 1853 Frye returned to Huntsville from one of his painting trips. He opened a studio on the west side of the square in a room formerly occupied by Governor Clay as a law office. This office would have been on Eustis Avenue across the street from the Church of the Nativity Episcopal.

IN 1865, the legislature of Kentucky resolved to have a full-length portrait of Henry Clay painted. They invited artists to compete for the honor, many of which entered the competition. The committee awarded the Palm of Excellence to the portrait painted by Frye. Governor Bramlette wrote Frye: "Your portrait of Henry Clay is a complete success, and has my full approval." He received $3,000, and the portrait hung over the speaker's chair in the Senate chamber. It now exists at the Kentucky Historical Society.

At the beginning of this short story, I mentioned that people had portraits painted before photography was invented. William Frye painted during a time that photography was more commonplace. He painted portraits from daguerreotypes as well as in-person sittings.

Surely this made portrait painting easier and made him more prolific when he didn't have to work at the whims of his live model. Painting from a photograph also allowed him to paint portraits posthumously.

Towards the very end of the 1860s, things started to change for Frye. His paintings had become distorted, and he could not tell if anything was wrong with them.

In early 1870, Frye traveled to Arkansas and painted a portrait of the founder of the Arkansas Gazette, William E. Woodruff, and his wife. These and other Arkansas portraits were the last ones he would produce. Later that year, he suffered a stroke in Memphis, giving him some form of paralysis. During a trip to Mobile in March 1871, he suffered yet another stroke.

After these strokes, he developed violent behavior. That fall, his wife wrote to Dr. Peter Bryce at the Alabama Insane Hospital in Tuscaloosa, later called Bryce Hospital, and she had her husband committed. A doctor and jury judged him a lunatic and indigent. He died in Tuscaloosa on July 1, 1872, at the age of 49, and was buried on the hospital grounds.

William Frye came to America for an adventure to see and paint the Indians and land-

Courtesy of HMCPL Special Collections

This portrait of Alabama Governor Clement Comer Clay is highly suspected to be by William Frye but not confirmed.

scapes of the west. Instead, he found a new adventure by raising a family and becoming a successful portrait painter in Huntsville, Alabama.

He did get to paint landscapes. His paintings of Huntsville's Big Spring and others from Alabama's black belt region are well known.

He painted over 140 known paintings, including the two that hang over the mantel in my parent's house.

WILLIAM FRYE,
PORTRAIT PAINTER,

HAS removed his Studio to the tenement heretofore occupied by Mr. J. Clemens, back of Lowe's corner, where he will be happy to exhibit to the ladies and gentlemen of Huntsville and vicinity specimens of his work.   *April* 6, 1845.

Advertisement in Huntsville's paper The Democrat

Clark Byers Sees Rock City

We had a "See Rock City" birdhouse in our backyard when I was growing up. It was painted red with a black roof with the words see rock city in white. I loved that birdhouse. When I grew up and lived in an apartment, I bought one for the small courtyard outside my front door. I don't think it ever had any birds living in it, but it had the right amount of kitsch and was a unique marker for those trying to find my apartment.

If you have lived in North Alabama, there is a good chance you have visited Chattanooga. If you have visited Chattanooga, then there is a good chance you went to see Rock City. Rock City Gardens was built on Lookout Mountain and features a 4,100-foot walking trail showcasing rock formations, caves, and lush gardens. Nearly a half-million people visit this attraction each year.

VALLEY HEAD ★

It all started with Garnet Carter, a businessman,

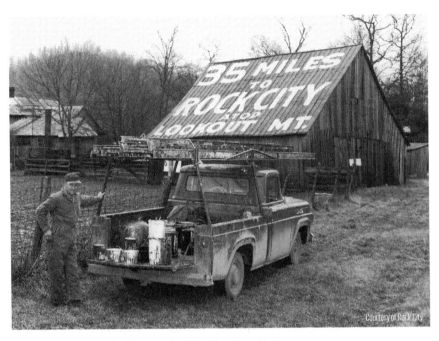

Clark Byers and the first barn he painted in 1936 on Hwy 41 near Chattanooga.

and developer who wanted to develop a residential neighborhood on Lookout Mountain, which overlooks Chattanooga. In 1924 he created a new community called Fairyland, and he wanted to cater to golfers who were flocking to the sport at the time. He built what is now known as the first miniature golf course in the U.S. He franchised his concept, and it became known as Tom Thumb golf.

While Carter worked on his golf concept, his wife Frieda took on a project of her own. The development of what would become Rock City Gardens.

The gardens opened in 1932 but promoting it was difficult at the time. Garnet came up with an idea. He hired Clark Byers to travel the nation's highways and offer to paint a farmer's barn in exchange for letting him paint three simple words: See Rock City. The black-and-white signs appeared as far north as Michigan and as far west as Texas. When the campaign started, more and more travelers were hitting the highways as the great depression was ending. His barns were beacons in the night to Americans looking for things to do and places to go. The campaign was a success as more and more travelers visited Rock City Gardens.

Our barn painter, Clark Byers, was born in 1915 in Flatrock in Northeast Alabama. By the time he was 15, his family had moved just across the state line to Georgia. He would spend his life rotating between Alabama, Georgia, and Tennessee but never moving too far in either direction.

Byers was a 22-year-old, self-taught painter working at a Chattanooga ad agency when Carter approached him with a job offer. He told Byers what barns to paint based on notes he made driving up and down U.S. Highway 41, a major north-south highway through Chattanooga.

The usual arrangement was that the barn owner would receive complimentary passes to Rock City and promotional items like Rock City thermometers, bath mats, or maybe even a birdhouse. And of course, the barn painting and touch-ups were free. If a farmer needed extra convincing, they might be paid a modest sum of $3, as well.

Byers would paint on the side of the barn and the pitched roof. He would freehand the lettering and then paint with a four-inch brush. There were no rollers back then. In time, he could paint or touch up as many as three barns a day.

Byers painted around 900 barns in 19 states until 1968 when President Lyndon Johnson sent him into retirement. Johnson saw outdoor boards as an eyesore rather than an icon. The "Ladybird Act" was legislation that banned billboards, and the See Rock City rooftop messages had to be removed. But luckily, some have survived.

It was probably just as well for Byers. He had dodged other hazards in the past, including slippery roofs, lightning, and a charging bull. About that same time, he was seriously electrocuted. Accounts are differing, but he was on a metal roof when it came in contact with an electrical wire, sending 7,000 volts through his body. And yes, he did survive.

Clark Byers has another connection to Alabama. After decades of painting barns for Rock City Gardens, the tourist attraction bug must have bit Byers hard.

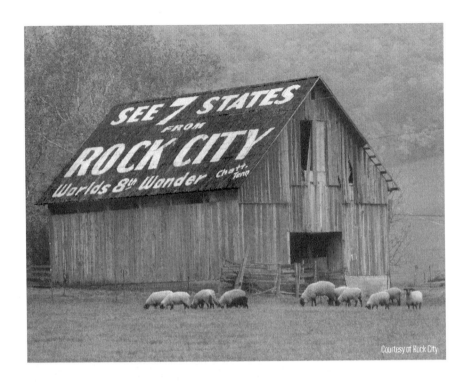

Courtesy of Rock City

In 1964, Byers and his partner Alva Hammond leased the Ellis Cave in Valley Head, Alabama. A popular local attraction, the developers saw potential in the cave, which was located right off U.S. Highway 11, a major north-south route through the eastern united states.

He renamed the cave Sequoyah Caverns, named after the famed Cherokee scholar who invented an alphabet for his nation. It's not known if Sequoyah ever visited the caves, but he did live in a village south of the property.

To make his cave different from others, he promoted the "looking glass lakes" within the cavern that reflected the surrounding stalactites and stalagmites.

Byers took his barn marketing knowledge to promote the caverns. In some cases, he would paint one side of the barn with See Rock City and the other promoting Sequoyah Caverns. And in a nod to his employer, he would call the caverns the ninth wonder of the world—the eighth is Rock City.

His time with Sequoyah Caverns was cut short when he was electrocuted.

The incident that I mentioned earlier. It took him a year to recover, and he was no longer able to work and keep up with the payments on the caverns. Rock City assumed the lease for their long-time and loyal employee. They took over the operations in March 1969. While Byers recuperated, he remained as part of the board of directors.

Promotion of Sequoyah Caverns on barns continued well into the 1980s, and they rivaled the number of Billboards for Rock City along the I-59 corridor between Gadsden and Chattanooga.

Out of the 900 barns painted with the See Rock City slogan, it is estimated that less than 100 exist today. Of those, only about ten are in Alabama.

Byers lived out his life in the Northeast Georgia town of Rising Fawn. One I-59 exit from Alabama. He tended cattle and cut hay, but he never did own a barn with the iconic See Rock City slogan on the roof, but his front yard did have a See Rock City birdhouse.

Clark Byers passed away at the age of 89 in 2004. He was buried in the Sulpher Springs Cemetery in Valley Head, Alabama, close to Sequoyah Caverns.

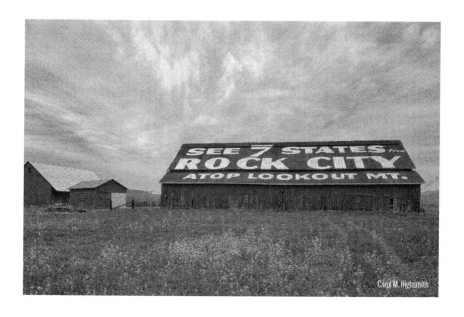

Carol M. Highsmith

▲ THE ARTISTS

Douglas Leigh Lights Up Times Square

The outdoor board has been ubiquitous around the state of Alabama. Signs are found up and down the interstate, in our towns, on back roads, and in every imaginable place. One of the most prolific users is Alexander Shunnarah, whose image can be seen on boards across the state. He is not alone; his many out-of-state competitors can be seen using the outdoor board to advertise their services as they try to keep up with Shunnarah.

Outdoor advertising is not popular with many people, and the state of Alabama has taken it on with Alabama code section 23-1-270, also known as the "Highway Beautification Act," which set limits on where these boards could be placed.

While some boards may be tacky without much thought put into them, some are pretty creative. For instance, Chik-fil-a has a series of 3D cows hanging from and playfully vandalizing boards asking the view-

Camel Man blew smoke rings every four seconds.

er to "eat more chikin'." I have always enjoyed the creativity put into some of these boards. But what makes an outboard board really stand out are lights. And when I think of lights, I think of Times Square in New York City.

But first, a little history before we get to the "Great White Way."

The original Native American inhabitants of Manhattan island created the Wickquasgeck trail. When the Dutch arrived, they widened the trail, making it the main thoroughfare through the island. The trail was renamed Broadway when the British took over. And this is why Broadway meanders through the city in defiance of the streets around it.

As New York City grew, a plan was needed for an orderly layout of streets. The New York State legislature stepped in and appointed a commission. The Commissioner's Plan of 1811 established a layout of grids or "gridiron" of roads throughout the borough. Broadway was left as is, which created a unique bow-tie space at the intersection with 7th Avenue. It is five blocks long between 42nd and 47th Streets. Originally known as Longacre Square, it was renamed Times Square in 1904 after the New York Times relocated its office to the newly constructed Times Building. It is now known as One Times Square, and you would know it as the building where the ball drops each New Year's Eve.

This urban canyon was a great place to advertise to the thousands of people walking past daily. Theaters, music halls, and upscale hotels moved into the area and after World War 1, Times Square, and the advertising boards located there, grew dramatically. And some of its more creative and memorable boards would come from the creativity of an Alabama native.

Douglas Leigh was born in Anniston, Alabama, in 1907. He always had a knack for selling things as a youth. He first left Alabama to attend the University of Florida, and to pay his way through college; he sold advertising for the yearbook. He bought all the advertising space in the yearbook for $2,000 on credit and then resold it for $7,000, making a $5,000 profit. To give you an idea of how much he made, it is over $80,000 today. The allure of doing so well with sales must have been overwhelming. He dropped out of school to work for the General Outdoor Advertising Company.

Sources say that he worked in Birmingham, where his parents had moved while he was in college. The 1930 census shows him living in a boarding house in Atlanta. He certainly could have worked in both cities as General Outdoor had of-

fices across the country. That is how he got to New York, transferring there in 1931.

The depression was taking its toll on the company, and Leigh had his salary cut five times during the short time he had been with the company in New York. When they gave him the sixth cut, he quit and set out on his own. Douglas Leigh Inc. opened

Douglas Leigh making a presentation.

The former Longacre Square South, renamed Times Square for the Times Building in the center of the photo.

its doors on March 4, 1933. A profile of Leigh in The New Yorker called him "perhaps the only person in the United States besides President Roosevelt who is now in charge of a going business that officially got underway on March 1933."

His company was located in the Bronx, but as they say, location is everything. He needed to be closer to the action. Leigh offered to design a sign for the St. Moritz Hotel. And instead of asking for cash, which would have been difficult for the St. Moritz at that time. He exchanged his services for the right to live there.

This barter allowed him to use the hotel's upscale address at 50 Central Park South for his business. Leigh then proceeded to transform the signs at Times Square, and by 1937 his firm was the second largest of its kind in the U.S.

His first eye-catching creation was in 1933. The billboard featured a coffee mug with real steam coming out of the top. He sold the space to the grocery chain A&P to advertise the store's Eight O'Clock Coffee. He seemed to have found his niche with this sign. Big, bright, bold, and creative enough to stand out from the competition all around him, even himself. He dubbed this new type of sign "spectacular." It started a new era of signage in Times Square.

One of Leigh's most iconic signs was for Camel Cigarettes. Artkraft Strauss was a leading sign company in Times Square, and they anticipated the onset of World War II. And they knew that the lights would have to go out during wartime or Times Square and the city would become an easy target for enemy bombers. They were looking for ways to attract attention without the neon and light bulbs.

Leigh's solution was to feature "Camel Man," and the sign was installed on the Claridge Hotel's facade in 1941. Every four seconds, from 7 am to 1 am, a perfect "o" of smoke would be exhaled from Camel Man's mouth, using steam from the hotel heating system. Over the next 25 years, the image of Camel Man would change until the sign came down in 1966. Interestingly, two years before the sign came down, Leigh purchased the Claridge Hotel in hopes of repurposing it for commercial and retail space.

Bond Clothes took over a two-story building between 44th and 45th street. Leigh convinced the owners to build an enormous sign 90 feet high and the length of the entire building. He created a waterfall in the sign that used 10,000 gallons of circulating water pumped over the falls every minute by 23 giant pumps on the roof. The waterfall was 27 feet high and 132 feet long and was flanked by two 50-foot tall figures. They seemed naked during the day but were clothed in lights at night.

In 1954, after just six years, Leigh made a proposition to Bond Clothes to allow other companies to use the sign space. They agreed, and Pepsi Cola took it over. The two human figures became Pepsi Cola bottles, and the clock was replaced with a giant bottle cap with the Pepsi logo on it. And, of course, the waterfall stayed.

During Douglas Leigh's long career, he designed around 78 spectaculars. Some of his more notable signs include:

A sign for Ballantine Beer that featured a giant Clown pitching quoits onto a

One of the blimps that Leigh obtained from the US Navy.

peg. The quoit, or ring, was in the shape of Ballantine's three-ring logo.

Wilson Whiskey's sign was 4,000 feet of display space, 100 miles of wire, and 10,000 light bulbs.

Kool cigarettes featured a winking penguin that stood on a mound of ice.

There was an animated cartoon for Old Gold cigarettes that had 4,100 bulbs.

Bromo-Seltzer had actual effervescent action, better known to us as bubbles.

And keeping with the bubble theme, Super Suds detergent had "floating" soap bubbles.

There was a 40-foot-high beer bottle and goblet, which was filled from a tap.

At the Loew Mayfair Building on 47th and 48th, Leigh created a sign for Schaefer Beer. He used the corner of the building in his design. Two 55-foot glasses touched in a toast at the corner of the building.

He even ventured outside of Times Square. A Coca-Cola sign on Columbus Circle gave an ever-changing weather forecast featuring a house and pictures of the sun, rain, snow, etc. The featured slogan was, "Thirst knows no season."

And Leigh went above and beyond the call of duty. When one woman kept hanging her laundry in front of one of his signs, he paid for her weekly laundry bills to keep her from doing it.

He had a dream to turn the Empire State Building into a giant cigarette ad for Lucky Strike. He proposed that the very top "mooring mast" would be the glowing end of the cigarette with smoke rising into the heavens. This ultimate "spectacular" almost happened when at the last minute, building owners came to their senses and decided against it.

He did get his chance to work on the Empire State Building. In 1976 he designed the wildly popular red, white and blue lighting for the country's bicentennial.

He designed lights for the tops of New York skyscrapers such as Citicorp, the Helmsley and Crown Buildings, and the Waldorf-Astoria Hotel.

After World War II, Leigh leased surplus blimps from the Navy. He painted the blimps for daytime viewing and installed lights for nighttime viewing. He used the blimps to advertise for clients such as Ford, Wonder Bread, Mobil gasoline, and MGM, which promoted its upcoming feature, National Velvet.

Remember the Times Building, which eventually became One Times Square? Leigh bought it in the 1960s, stripped the marble from the building, and turned it into a showcase for signs, which is what it is today.

In 1984, Leigh designed and illuminated a large, 17 ft. by 14 ft. snowflake with 3,000 lights and over 12,000 crystals. This snowflake hung over the intersection of Fifth Avenue and 57th Street every holiday season, starting in 1984. It has since been replaced with a newer snowflake. This one was designed by Baccarat and is now known as the UNICEF Crystal Snowflake.

Douglass Leigh died at the age of 92 in a Manhattan Hospital. The next time you are in Times Square, look around and remember that a son of Anniston, Alabama had a vision (was a billboard visionary) for Times Square that gave New York its visual identity to this day.

Part 8

THE INVENTORS

What differentiates us mortal people from inventors
is that when we encounter a problem, we sidestep it
and move on with our lives. An inventor will try
and come up with a way to solve that problem.
Alabama has its share of inventors, and the ones
featured in this section come from all walks of life.
Each had to overcome hurdles society threw in
front of them while they were solving the problem.

Mary Anderson - Inventor of the Windshield Wiper

I had always wanted a Fiat 124 Spider convertible. When the opportunity to purchase one for cheap came up, I blindly jumped at the chance. It needed a lot of TLC. I didn't realize it when I bought it, but I didn't have the skills or money to get it back into pristine shape. I dumped too much money into it in an attempt to fix it. I drove it every day, except when it rained. The windshield wiper motor did not work, and on this 1968 Fiat, no amount of money was going to fix it. You can do many things in the rain, but if you don't have working windshield wipers, you can't drive. Luckily I found a buyer for that Fiat.

We take the windshield wiper for granted. As the saying goes, "you don't miss it until they're gone." Speaking of which, you might be surprised to learn that the windshield wiper was invented here in Alabama.

Mary Anderson was born on Burton Hill Plantation in Greene County on February 19, 1866, to

Mary Anderson

John and Rebecca Anderson. Unfortunately, Mary's father passed away when she was four years old. Burton Hill Plantation had 3,000 acres of land and must have been challenging to manage as a single mother with two young children. It is unknown how long they managed the plantation and if and when they sold it. But we know that Mary, her sister Frances, and her mother eventually moved to Main Street in Eutaw, Alabama, where the girls went to school, and the estate's proceeds supported the family.

The proceeds must have been substantial, for in 1889, when Mary was 23, the three women moved to Birmingham and the Fairmont Apartments at 1211 21st Street South on the southeast corner of Highland Avenue. An apartment building they had built.

For those familiar with Birmingham, The 2101 Highland Avenue building is the location of the former Fairmont Apartments. It is a seven-story building with a large modern sculpture out front. On the southeast corner, South Highland Presbyterian Church built a new sanctuary there, and the congregation moved in 1892. Across Highland Avenue on the Northeast corner would be Temple Emmanuel, which was built in 1912.

In 1889, this was the town of Highlands. Birmingham was just 19 years old, and this area of Jones Valley was on a ridge just south of the new city. Well-to-do citizens were moving there to get away from Birmingham with all its heat, noise, dirt, and malaria.

The location for the apartment was prime land and probably a good investment for the Anderson women. The Highland town hall was on the Northwest corner of the intersection where Highland Manor apartments are now.

But back to our story.

The entrepreneur gene must have been strong in the Anderson women. To have continued to operate the plantation after the death of the patriarch, John Anderson, is impressive enough. Then to build an apartment building in a booming Birmingham is impressive.

Soon after moving to Birmingham, sister Frances, better known as Fannie, wed George Perrin Thornton, who was born in Greene County and then moved with his family to California a few years after the civil war. I am not sure of his story and how he and Fannie got together, but they did. They got married in 1891 and had a daughter, Rebecca, who was born in Arizona the following year.

Mary left Birmingham in 1893, at the age of 27. She moved to Fresno, California, and operated a cattle ranch and vineyard. We have already established that Mary was an entrepreneur, and seeing that she was unmarried, she needed to find her path in life away from her family. Even still, the leap from apartment owner to cattle rancher seems a stretch.

It seems that her new brother-in-law George was a cattleman, and his family was in Fresno. Making the transition a bit easier and not so random. Cattle ranching is another explanation of why George and Fannies' daughter Rebecca was born in Arizona.

Mary spent five years in California and returned to Birmingham in 1898 to help care for an ailing aunt.

By this time, the whole family was living at the Fairmont Apartments. Fannie, George, and Rebecca had also moved back to Birmingham. It seems that the Fair-

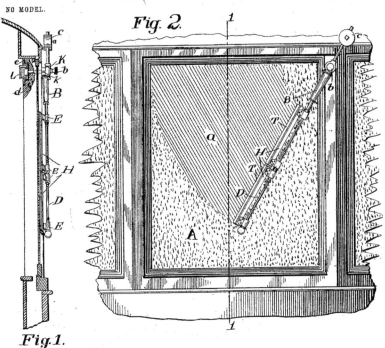

Fig. 2.

Fig. 1.

mont hosted many Anderson relatives throughout the years.

Mary's ailing aunt brought 17 trunks with her, and they all stayed in her room, not letting any out of her sight. Once a week, Mary would open the trunks and remove the trays so that her aunt could try on the enclosed items and look at herself. She was maybe dreaming of a time past. The only rule was that Mary had to close her eyes and not look at what was in the trunks. When her aunt died, Mary inherited the trunks. She found the trays filled with jewels, gold, and other treasures.

Using some of the money from her newfound wealth, Mary took a trip to New York City in the winter of 1902. It was cold, and the wind drove the snow straight down the man-made canyons of the city. Mary stood on a corner and watched a streetcar stop, the motorman get out, wipe the snow off the windshield, get back in, and move down the street until the window was covered and the process repeated itself.

Mary wondered why there wasn't some mechanical way that the window could clear itself of snow. She learned that methods had tried and failed. Such as using the juice from a plug of tobacco, half an onion, and a carrot. None of which cleared the snow. All it did was leave the windshield a mess.

The best the streetcar engineers could come up with was to split the window in half so that the motorman could open one side, reach out and clear the other window. This solution kept him from having to get out of the car, but the downside was it gave the passengers a shot of cold, wet, wind, and snow.

She came back to Birmingham, but the image of that motorman having to clean the window would not leave her head. What if, she thought, there was some arm on the outside of the streetcar. Would it clean off the window while the motorman stayed inside the car?

Mary worked on her design with an arm on the outside that was operated by an internal crank. She took her plan to a Birmingham manufacturing company that made a working model for her.

A local attorney applied for a patent in her name, and on November 10, 1903, patent number 743801 was issued to Mary Anderson for her invention of the windshield wiper.

Now it was time to get to work and make some money.

In 1905 she wrote to the Montreal company Dinning and Eckenstein to find if they were interested in purchasing her patent. In their return letter, it stated:

"We beg to acknowledge receipt of your recent favor with reference to the sale of your patent. In reply, we regret to state we do not consider it to be of such commercial value as would warrant our undertaking its sale."

What a missed opportunity. It wouldn't be the last.

Was it the fact that so many people did not see value in the early part of the century? Or was it the fact that this unmarried, independent woman was presenting a product in a business world run by men who discounted her the minute they met her? Could be.

We also need to look back at the year. Mary's windshield wiper was for the streetcar. Automobiles were very new at the time. Ford produced the Model A between 1903 and 1905, and it didn't even have a windshield.

Eventually, she gave up the battle against a perceived lack of demand for windshield wipers and stopped trying to sell it.

By 1920, the prevalence of cars on the road had skyrocketed, and the industry came around to her ideas. Based on her designs, Windshield wipers became a standard feature on vehicles. Cadillac was the first to install them in 1922.

Unfortunately, In 1920, Mary's patent on the windshield wiper had expired, and she never made a dime.

In the years after, Mary lived in Birmingham and would spend summers in Monteagle, Tennessee. Her mother died in 1924, and her sister, Fannie, died in 1933, whose own husband, George, had died 20 years before.

Mary Anderson died of a cerebral hemorrhage on June 27, 1953, at the Monteagle Assembly Grounds. She was buried in Birmingham at Elmwood Cemetery. She had been a member of South Highlands Presbyterian Church and, at the time of her death, was the oldest living member, joining soon after the church was founded.

Fortunately, Mary Anderson and her contributions to the automotive industry did not go unnoticed. She was inducted into the National Inventors Hall of Fame in 2011.

The story is over, but I know you're dying to hear about the Fiat. The car I was talking about at the beginning of this episode. About a year after I sold the car, I found it parked along Highland Avenue, not far from Mary Anderson's former residence. There was a sign on it that said: "For Sale, make me an offer." I guess the owner realized that even he couldn't drive without windshield wipers.

◢ THE INVENTORS

Andrew Jackson Beard - Inventor of the Janey Coupler

Have you ever been stuck at a railroad crossing? The longer you sit there, waiting for the train to pass, it seems as if the train goes slower and slower. And the trains seem to be getting longer and longer. One of the largest passenger trains in the United States was the Ringling Brothers and Barnum and Bailey Circus train which had almost 60 cars. A coal train ran from West Virginia to Ohio in 1967 that had 500 cars and six locomotives. It's not the length of these trains that stands out to me unless you are stuck waiting at a railroad crossing. The effort it takes to get these cars in the correct order and stay connected is remarkable.

BIRMINGHAM

This process happens at railroad yards across the country, and you would be forgiven if you've never seen one. They seem to be hidden away, just on the other side of a fence or row of buildings. A railroad yard is a huge area with a series of parallel tracks used to unload freight and sort and store cars waiting to be assembled

Andrew Jackson Beard

into a train.

Each of those cars needs to be connected by a linkage such as a link and pin coupler. This was the original style used in North America. If you look at the end of each of these early cars, you would see what looked to be a rectangle box with a slot in it. A link, imagine one piece of a large chain, would go in the slot, and a pin would be inserted from the top, securing that side of the link. The other side of the link would then be attached to the next car. A worker would stand between the cars as they came together, and he would insert the pin at just the right moment into the other hole connecting the two cars.

My description may be hard to imagine, but know that this was a dangerous job. At the least, a worker would lose a finger, or two, or maybe an entire hand because they did not get the pin in place at the right time. Some workers were crushed between two cars or would get dragged underneath.

It wasn't a great solution, even if you took out the gruesome injuries and deaths associated with the link and pin system.

There was no nationwide standard design, which added time to linking up cars, and as cars increased in size, the link and pin system couldn't hold up. A better link was needed.

Andrew Jackson Beard was born a slave on a plantation near Mt. Pinson in

Jefferson County in 1849. He gained his freedom when the Emancipation Proclamation was issued when he was 15 years old, and he married his wife Edie Beard when he was 16 years old. They would go on to have three children. Beard and his family took their surname from the owners of the plantation. Even though he was a free man, he stayed on the plantation until he was 18 years old.

Beard was a farmer for the next five years. After a difficult trip to Montgomery to sell fifty bushels of apples that took three weeks, Beard quit farming. It was just too labor-intensive.

Next, he became a millwright in St. Claire County, where he built and ran a flour mill. But even that couldn't satisfy a man like Andrew Beard. Even though he could not read or write, not even write his name, Beard had a mechanical mind and was constantly tinkering with the tools of his trade and finding ways to improve them.

He wondered how he could improve on the common plow he had worked with for so long. In 1881, he improved and patented plans for a double blade plow with adjustable blades. He sold the rights to his design for $4,000 just a few years later. To put that into perspective, that would be like receiving over $100,000 today. In 1887 he sold the rights to an even more improved plow for $5,200.

From slave to an inventor in a short 17 years was a remarkable feat. Not only did he patent his inventions, but he also made money from them, which is not always the case with inventors. In our season 1 story about Mary Anderson, inventor of the windshield wiper, she never made a dime from her invention.

At the time of his second patent, Beard lived in the Woodlawn area of Birmingham and invested his newfound wealth into a profitable real-estate business.

Beard was not done inventing. He received two patents for rotary steam engines in 1890 and 1892 before turning his attention to improving the railroad industry. Word of Beard's mechanical abilities had spread, and he had started receiving offers of employment from competing companies.

As I mentioned earlier, coupling railcars was dangerous, and there was even

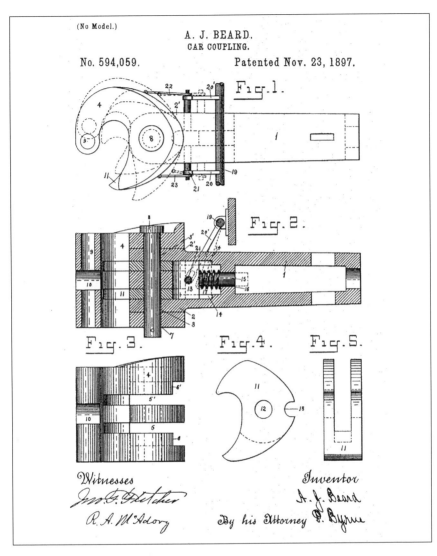

A. J. BEARD.
CAR COUPLING.

No. 594,059.   Patented Nov. 23, 1897.

Fig.1.

Fig.2.

Fig.3.   Fig.4.   Fig.5.

Witnesses

Jno. G. Fletcher

R. A. McAdory

Inventor

A. J. Beard

By his Attorney P. Byrne

Jackson's first patent for the automatic train car coupler

mention that Beard was seriously injured and had lost a leg. I could not find proof for this, but I am sure Beard saw enough injuries that he was moved to improve upon the coupling system.

Beard designed what is called a knuckle coupler, also known as a Janney Coupler. The Janney coupler, also pronounced as a jenny coupler, was initially created

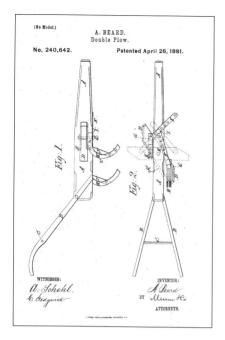
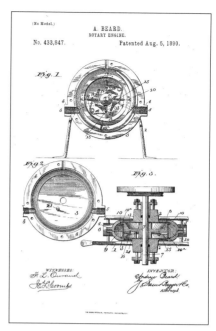

Jackson's patents for a double plow (left) and a rotary engine (right).

in 1873 by Eli Janney, and improved versions of this style of coupler are in use to this day.

Three of those improved versions of the Janney coupler were designed by Beard. His first patent was granted in 1897, and his improvement was that the couplers automatically locked. This was the first coupler that automatically locked in the United States. His coupler would connect with the existing Janney coupler and was cheaper to manufacture and fix if broken. The same year his patent was granted, the U.S. Congress passed the Federal Safety Appliance Act, making it illegal to operate any railroad car without automatic couplers. Timing is everything, as they say.

He made improvements to his design with patents in 1897 and 1905, and he founded the Beard Automatic Coupler Company to market his product. Beard sold the patent rights to his Janney coupler for $50,000, just shy of 1.5 million dollars today.

The sales and royalties from his patents and investments in other businesses made Andrew Jackson Beard the first African American millionaire in Jefferson County. You would assume that he would go on and live out his life in some form of luxury or comfort, but that wouldn't be the case. Little is known about the last decade of his life, other than he became paralyzed and impoverished. The 1920 census has him listed as an inmate at the Jefferson County Almshouse. An almshouse was generally a house of last resort for the poor, disabled, and elderly.

He died May 10, 1921, and is buried in Greenwood Cemetery in an unmarked grave.

Andrew Jackson Beard was recognized for his work and was posthumously inducted into the National Inventors Hall of Fame in 2006 in recognition of his revolutionary Jannie coupler.

So the next time you are stuck at a railroad crossing watching the cars slow down in front of you, take a look at the couplers and know that a man from Alabama, a former slave named Andrew Jackson Beard, had a vital hand in creating them.

John Pratt - Inventor of the Typewriter

By far, the most helpful class I took at Homewood High School in the late 1970s was typing. Little did I know that most of the work that I would do would be on a computer a short decade later. We used the IBM Selectric typewriter in typing class, which was an awesome machine. Earlier typewriters had letters on individual typebars that swung up to strike the ribbon. It was almost like a panicked spider was trying to claw its way out of the machine. The Selectric featured a typeball with all the letters on that one ball, and it would spin and strike the paper as it would glide across the roller, typing your words. The IBM Selectric would capture 75% of the market before personal computers would make the typewriter irrelevant.

CENTRE ★

In high school, we were taught how to touch-type, where each finger has its own key on the keyboard. We were taught the home position with left-hand fingers on A, S, D & F. Right hand would be on J, K, L &

Alabama Department of Archives and History

John Pratt

the semicolon. Both thumbs would be used to move the space bar. Have you noticed the raised part of your keyboard's F and J keys? It's so touch-typers will know by feel when they are on the correct keys.

Typing class has turned into keyboarding, and it was taught to my children in middle school. I am not sure if they learned to touch-type, but my son is a wiz at the hunt and peck method and using his thumbs on his mobile phone. I can't type unless the keyboard is right in front of me and my posture is correct.

Now I write left-handed, and I can only describe my handwriting style as a monkey with a crayon. It's not pretty and can be uncomfortable over time. When writing, left-handers push the pen across the page, whereas right-handers pull the pen across the page, and that makes a big difference. My palm was coated with graphite in school after a big day of writing with a pencil.

Over the centuries, others must have struggled with this problem as well. Not that they are lefthanded, but they probably realized it would make their life easier to have a mechanical way to write.

The earliest known typing instrument goes back as far as the 16th century, and as business grew in the 19th century, the need for a typewriter type device was apparent. Historians have estimated that some form of the typewriter has been

Typewriter invented in 1864.

invented at least 52 times. And one of those was by John Pratt of Alabama.

John Pratt was born in Union, South Carolina, on April 14, 1831, and moved to Alabama with his father's family as a young man. He married, practiced law, was a reporter, and taught school. Later he was part owner and editor of the paper in Centre, Alabama.

As a writer, lawyer, and teacher, he spent a lot of time writing. He was writing with the tools of the time, pen and ink, and during his time as a registrar, he suffered from hand cramps. I can only imagine that Pratt dreamed of a way to write

Later model of the typewriter

more comfortably. Not only did he start to dream about just such a machine, but he also put the dream into action.

He got together with a local printer named John Neely, who fashioned some type he thought would work. Pratt put together the machine. By 1860 he was routinely using it for correspondence, court, and writing editorials.

He wanted to develop his machine further, but he could see that war was coming to Alabama. He sold his possessions and moved to England to further develop his typewriter.

On December 1, 1866, Pratt received a British Patent for a writing machine called a "ptereotype." He exhibited his typewriter before the Society of Arts, The Society of Engineers in London, and the Royal Society of Great Britain. At that time, it was the most complete and practical typewriter developed.

The Royal British Scientific Society printed an account of the machine, reprinted in the July 6, 1867 issue of Scientific American magazine. In the article titled "Type Writing Machine," the article begins: "A machine by which it is assumed that a man may print his thoughts twice as fast as he can write them and with the advantage of the legibility, compactness, and neatness of print, has lately been exhibited before the London Society of Arts by the inventor, Mr. Pratt, of Alabama..."

Pratt was able to sell his typewriter in London, and because of the success, he moved back to the United States in 1868 and received a U.S. Patent that same year.

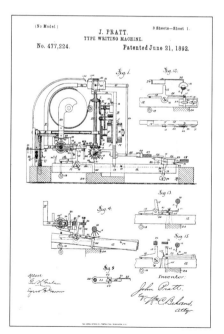 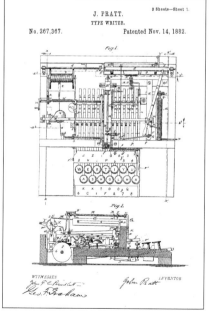

Patents for two of his later model typewriters

In 1866, Christopher Sholes of Milwaukee designed a machine that printed page numbers in books, serial numbers on tickets, and anything else that needed a number. A friend and fellow inventor Carlos Glidden had read the article in Scientific American about Pratt's ptereotype, and he thought the machine was too complicated but could be improved. Glidden asked Sholes about his printer, "if numbers, why not letters?"

An editorial in the same issue of Scientific America probably helped motivate Christopher Sholes by pointing out "the great benefit to mankind which such a machine would confer, as well as the fortune that awaited the successful inventor."

Sholes and his partners would develop the Remington typewriter, which is the closest to what we know as the modern typewriter with the QWERTY keyboard. The first Remington typewriter was sold in 1874.

Pratt continued to invent. He obtained a second patent for a "type wheel," which he sold to James Hammond in 1882, becoming part of the Hammond typewriter. In the 1890s, he became the Hammond Type Writing Company superintendent in New York. In 1902 he moved to Chattanooga to be closer to his sisters, and he died there in 1905. He is buried at Pratt Memorial Park, which is close to Centre, Alabama

If you want to see Pratt's ptereotype, one surviving machine is on exhibit at the Victoria and Albert Museum in London, England.

John Pratt may not have invented the typewriter as you and I know it, but that's ok. I like what one published article said: "*if Sholes is called the father of the typewriter, then Pratt may justly be called the grandfather.*"

Notes on Sources

THE ICONS

MISS LIBERTY - BIRMINGHAM'S STATUE

Beiman, Irving, "Miss Liberty is Coming." *The Birmingham News* (8 Sep 1957): Page 111

"A Ten-Ton Lady Rides the Southern" http://southern.railfan.net/ties/1958/58-10/lady.html

"Liberty National Statue." Bhamwiki.com. https://www.bhamwiki.com/w/Liberty_National_statue

Staff writer, "Statue of Liberty Model Coming Here." *The Birmingham News*. 2 July 1952: Page 17

"Statue of Liberty, Pont de Grenelle." *Atlas Obscura*. 3 December 2015. https://www.atlasobscura.com/places/statue-of-liberty-pont-de-grenelle

"Statue of Liberty on Ile aux Cygnes in Paris." https://www.eutouring.com/statue_of_liberty_paris.html

"Torchmark Corporation History." http://www.fundinguniverse.com/company-histories/torchmark-corporation-history/

PHOTOS

"Miss Liberty in Liberty Park" by Shawn Wright

"Workers with statue on Ground and Miss Liberty being raised to the roof of the Liberty National Building." Alabama Department of Archives and History. Donated by Alabama Media Group. Photo by Roy Carter or Robert Adams, Birmingham News.

VULCAN'S TORCH

"About." Birmingham Jaycees. https://bhamjaycees.wordpress.com/about/

Duncan, Andy Alabama. *Curiosities: Quirky Characters, Roadside Oddities & Other Offbeat Stuff*: Globe Pequot Press, 2009

"Giuseppe Moretti." *Bhamwiki.org.* https://www.bhamwiki.com/w/Giuseppe_Moretti

Glionna, John. "Birmingham's Vulcan statue, often the butt of jokes, remains well-loved." *Los Angeles Times.* 12 April 2015.

House, Jack. "Vulcan keeps watch, his torch tells the story" *The Birmingham News.* 4 Nov 1951: Page 29

Hillinger, Charles. "Alabama Statue Signals Traffic Deaths." *The Los Angeles Times.* 12 Oct 1984: Page 28

"Jaycee 'Safety Light' Fund Drives Speed." *The Birmingham News.* 14 Aug 1946: Page 15

"Moon Over Homewood." *Bhamwiki.com.* https://www.bhamwiki.com/w/Moon_Over_Homewood

"On this day in Alabama history: Vulcan's torch turns green for the first time." *Alabama News Center.* October 23, 2019. https://alabamanewscenter.com/2019/10/23/on-this-day-in-alabama-history-vulcans-torch-turns-green-for-the-first-time/

"Vulcan." *Bhamwiki.org.* https://www.bhamwiki.com/w/Vulcan

"Vulcan (mythology)." *Wikipedia.org.* https://en.wikipedia.org/wiki/Vulcan_(mythology)

"Vulcan's Torch." *Bhamwiki.com.* https://www.bhamwiki.com/w/Vulcan%27s_torch

PHOTOS

Underwood & Underwood, Copyright Claimant. Colossal iron statue of Vulcan, 56 ft. high, weight 100,000 lbs., in Mines Bldg., World's Fair, St. Louis, U.S.A. Saint Louis Missouri, ca. 1904. New York, N.Y.: Underwood &

Underwood. Photograph. https://www.loc.gov/item/95508072/.

Keystone View Company, Copyright Claimant. At the feet of old Vulcan, Palace of Mines and Metallurgy, Louisiana Purchase Exposition, St. Louis, Mo., U.S.A. Saint Louis Missouri, ca. 1905. [Meadville, Pa.: Keystone View Company, 1904] Photograph. https://www.loc.gov/item/95508082/.

"Statue in 2022 and Torch" by Shawn Wright

USS ALABAMA

"All out effort to be made to bring the USS Alabama back." *Abbeville Herald*. 7 May 1964: Page 1

"Bad Steering Gear Linked to Tug Loss." *New York Times*. 25 Aug 1964.

"Children's Campaign." USSAlabama.com. https://www.ussalabama.com/get-involved/foundation/

"Governor's Committee at work to 'Save the USS Alabama'." *Pickens County Herald and West Alabamian*. 1 Nov 1962: Page 10

"More Battleships Declared Obsolete" *The Berkshire Eagle*. 3 May 1962: Page 11

"Park Complete History." USSAlabama.com. http://www.ussalabama.com/park-complete-history/

"Skipper of ship through panama canal gives running account of trip." *The Mobile Journal*. 11 Sep 1964: Page 1

Todd Kreamer, Historian with the USS Alabama Battleship Memorial Park

"Tug Sinks in Canal." *New York Times*. 23 Aug 1964.

"The story of the USS Alabama." *The Phenix-Citizen Herald*. 14 May 1964: Page 2

"USS Alabama may resume trip soon." *The Selma Times-Journal*. 1 Sep 1964: Page 2

"USS Alabama Reaches 'Home.'" *The Florence Herald*. 17 Sep 1964: Page 1

"USS Alabama Sits At Anchor." *The Anniston Star*. 21 Oct 1962: Page 8

PHOTOS

Highsmith, Carol M, photographer. USS Alabama BB-60, Mobile Bay, Alabama. United States Alabama Mobile Bay, 2010. Photograph. https://www.loc.gov/item/2010637026/.

"Ex-USS Alabama (BB-60) is towed into Puget Sound on the start of her last voyage to Mobile, Alabama, where she will serve as a museum ship." L45-04.01.01 courtesy of the Naval History & Heritage Command.

428-GX-USN-1105620-C: Panama Canal Zone. USS Alabama (BB 60) moves through Gaillard (Culebra) Cut with tugs to port and stern. Photographed by Helrauth, August 26, 1964. Official U.S. Navy Photograph, now in the collections of the National Archives.

"USS Alabama arriving in Mobile Bay from Washinton state." Alabama Department of Archives and History. Donated by Alabama Media Group. Photo by Anthony Falletta, Birmingham News.

MISS FANCY

"Avondale Park" https://avondalepark.org/

"Avondale" *Bhamwiki.com*. https://www.bhamwiki.com/w/Avondale

"Avondale Mills" *Bhamwiki.com*. https://www.bhamwiki.com/w/Avondale_Mills

"Avondale Cave" *Bhamwiki.com*. https://www.bhamwiki.com/w/Avondale_Cave

"Avondale Zoo" *Bhamwiki.com*. https://www.bhamwiki.com/w/Avondale_Zoo

Beasley, Cecil. "Elephant No Prohibitionist, Especially when sick, trainer declares." *The Birmingham News*. 27 Aug 1930: Page 16

"Birmingham Zoo." *Wikipedia.org*. https://en.wikipedia.org/wiki/Birmingham_Zoo

"Came to this city and bought an elephant." *The Tuscaloosa News*. 9 Nov 1913: Page 1

"Children's elephant will be at the Avondale Zoo this afternoon." *Birmingham Age-Herald*. 13 Nov 1913: Page 1

"City Commission orders Avondale Zoo abolished as economy move" *Birmingham News* (8 Oct 1934)

Cole Bros.-Clyde Beaty Circus. 1934 Handbook. Fulton County, Indiana

Conway, Chris "She Was City's Pride" Birmingham Post-Herald. 15 July 1968:
    Page 8

"Elephant is quartered in stable for the time being" *The Birmingham News*. 10
    Nov 1913: Page 2

"Fancy is getting acquainted with animals at zoo" *Birmingham Age-Herald*. 13
    Nov 1913: Page 1

"Hagenbeck Wallace Circus" *Wikipedia.org*. https://en.wikipedia.org/wiki/

Hunter, Beth "Miss Fancy" *Encyclopedia of Alabama*. http://
    encyclopediaofalabama.org/article/h-4139

"John Todd" *Bhamwiki.com*. https://www.bhamwiki.com/w/John_Todd

"Miss Fancy Strolls" *The Birmingham News*. 12 Aug 1930: Page 6

"Miss Fancy, the pleasant elephant, has made children so happy that now there is
    discussion to increase the Birmingham Zoo." *Birmingham Age-Herald*.16 Nov
    1913: Page 6

"Sheppard Takes Fancy" *The Birmingham News*. 11 Nov 1913: Page 3

"Underground River" *Bhamwiki.com*. https://www.bhamwiki.com/w/
    Underground_river

PHOTOS

"Miss Fancy, with keeper, Dayton Allen." Alabama Department of Archives and
    History

"Two young women with Miss Fancy." 1556.60.90. Birmingham Public Library
    Archives

"Hagenbeck-Wallace Circus Poster." Library of Congress Prints and
    Photographs Division. http://hdl.loc.gov/loc.pnp/ppmsca.54934

THE FIRSTS

WSY, THE FIRST RADIO STATION IN ALABAMA

"Auburn Will Operate Powerful Radio Station in City of Birmingham." *The Auburn Alumnus Vol. X No. 2.* October 1928.

"Broadcasting room of Alabama Power Co. finest in the world, experts on acoustics say." *The Birmingham News.* 2 Oct 1922: Page 2

Burch, B.F. "Our Latest Broadcast Station." *Powergrams. Vol. IV. No. 2.* (May 1923): Pages 9-12

"Civitan Club is started by radio." *The Birmingham News.* 23 Dec 1922: Page 2

Miller, G.K. "Our Broadcasting Station" *Powergrams.* 1922: Page 23

"New studio WSY Alabama Power Co. Finest South." *The Montgomery Times.* 30 Sep 1922: Page 5

Rosene, James M. "Thesis for Master of Arts: The history of radio broadcasting at Auburn University (1912-1961)." 12 Dec 1968.

Southerland, J.S. "Listening In" *Powergrams.* July 1922: Pages 12-13

"Tiger-Tech game to be broadcast." *The Birmingham News.* 29 Nov 1922: Page 9

"The WAPI Story." *Alabama Historical Radio Society.*
Broken Link: https://www.alabamahistoricalradiosociety.org/Archives/
WAPI%20Radio%20%26%20Television/The%20WAPI%20Story.pdf

WAPI (AM). *Wikipedia.org.* https://en.wikipedia.org/wiki/WAPI_(AM)

WSY. *Bhamwiki.org.* https://www.bhamwiki.com/w/WSY

WSY Brochure celebrating 100 year anniversary designed by Shawn Wright. 1992

"WSY Sings Swan Song." *Powergrams.* November 1923: Page 18

PHOTOS

Image(s)/information courtesy of Alabama Power Company Corporate Archives.

THE CLUB AT THE END OF THE WORLD

Atkins, Leah Rawls. *"A History 1951-1986."* 1986

"Our History." *The Club Inc.org*. https://www.theclubinc.org/default.aspx
  p=DynamicModule&pageid=71&ssid=100072

"The Club." *Bhamwiki.org*. https://www.bhamwiki.com/w/The_Club

PHOTOS

"The Club sign and view of Birmingham" by Shawn Wright

THE FIRST 911 CALL

"911 Celebrates 25 Years." *The Muscatine Journal* (18 Jan 1993): Page 4

"9-1-1 Origin & History." National Emergency Number Association. https://
  www.nena.org/page/911overviewfacts

Duncan, Andy. *Alabama. Curiosities: Quirky Characters, Roadside Oddities & Other
  Offbeat Stuff*. Globe Pequot Press, 2009

"State Made First 911 Call." *The Montgomery Advertiser*. 23 Feb 2008: Page 13

"Town to celebrate first 911 service." The Montgomery Advertiser. 17 Jan 1993:
  Page 1

Yeager, Andrew. "50 Years Ago, How A Small Alabama Town Pioneered The
  First 911 Call." *Morning Edition, NPR*. 21 Feb 2018.
  https://www.npr.org/2018/02/21/587502641/50-years-ago-how-a-small-
  alabama-town-pioneered-the-first-911-call

PHOTO

"Hayleville 911 Center" by Ginger Ann Brook. deepfriedkudzu.com
Stock photo similar in style to original phone.

THE ATHLETES

BEAR BRYANT WANTS YOU TO CALL YOUR MAMA

Luckie & Forney Inc. Advertising. *Bear Bryant "call your momma" Commercial - South Central Bell*. https://youtu.be/eVfMuGVZcGI

"Robert Luckie, Jr." http://www.bhamwiki.com/w/Robert_Luckie

Wright, Shawn and Wright, Leo. "Bear Bryant Wants You to Call Your Mama." *Alabama Short Stories*. 20 April 2020. Produced by Shawn Wright. Podcast.

PHOTOS

Bear Bryant image is a screen grab from the South Central Bell Commercial. Script image by Shawn Wright

GREENVILLE BASKETBALL

"1921 AHSAA Basketball Tournament Champions" *AHSFHS.org*. http://www.ahsfhs.org/basketball/tournament1.asp?Year=1921

"Coach Brown's Springville Five Slips Old Man Dope Husky Kayo In Beating Greenville." *Birmingham News*. 26 Feb 1921.

"Greenville Coach Praised by B.A.C." *Birmingham News*. 13 Mar 1921.

"Greenville High Wins First Game." *The Greenville Advocate*. 25 Feb 1921: Page 1

"Greenville Team Wins Fifth Place." *The Greenville Advocate*. 1 Mar 1922: Page 1

"Local Five Ready for Birmingham Tourney." *The Greenville Advocate*. 22 Feb 1922: Page 1

Oral History from Rhetta Wright. Daughter of Skeeter McQueen. 2020.

PHOTOS

Basketball team courtesy of Rhetta McQueen Wright

Buildings in Birmingham. "Birmingham 1915" Birmingham Chamber of Commerce. In the public domain.

FOOTBALL IN THE COURTS

"Black Bears Taking ASHAA to State Court." *AP*, 7 Nov 1974.

"Gridder Happy About 'Birthday.'" *The Montgomery Advertiser.* 9 Nov 1974: Page 12

"Homewood may be back in state 4-A playoffs." *The Selma Times-Journal*, 14 Nov 1974: Page 8

"Homewood voted into 4-A playoffs." *AP*. 16 Nov 1974.

"Homewood Wins Battle" *AP*. 16 Nov 1974.

"Judge Rules for Homewood" *AP*, 14 Nov 1974.

Kirk, Patrick. *Fighting Patriots: The first three years of Homewood Football.* BookBaby.com. 2020.

"Reads like a soap opera" *The Montgomery Advertiser*, 21 Nov 1974: Page 47

"Will high court let AHSAA end playoff dispute?" *Alabama Journal.* 14 Nov 1974: Page 3

Wright, Shawn and Gross, Michael. "Michael Gross and Homewood High Athletics" 11 February 2020. *Shades Cahaba Oral History.* Podcast. https://shadescahabahistory.com/michael-gross-and-homewood-high-athletics/

Wright, Shawn and Kirkpatrick, Wade. "Wade Kirkpatrick, Fighting Patriots – Special Edition." 28 Jan 2020. *Shades Cahaba Oral History.* Podcast. https://shadescahabahistory.com/wade-kirkpatrick-fighting-patriots-special-edition/

* If you would like to know more about the Homewood Patriots 1974 Season, look for the book *Fighting Patriots: The first three years of Homewood Football* by Patrick Kirk. You can find it at https://store.bookbaby.com/book/fighting-patriots

PHOTOS

Homewood High School Yearbook 1974

GORDIE HOWE SCORES A GOAL

Bryan, Jimmy. "Milestone on ice: Howe's 1,000th goal" *The Birmingham News*. 8 Dec 1977.

Bryan, Jimmy. "Whalers win easily, 6-3,... and Howe" *The Birmingham News*. 8 Dec 1977.

Cargile, John. "1,000! Howe hits sports milestone." *Birmingham Post-Herald*. 8 Dec 1977.

"Gordie Howe." *Wikipedia.org*. https://en.wikipedia.org/wiki/Gordie_Howe

Proudfoot, Shannon. "The goalie who gave up Gordie Howe's 1000th goal." *McCleans*. 10 June 2016: https://www.macleans.ca/news/canada/the-goalie-who-gave-up-gordie-howes-1000th-goal/

Schwartz, Larry. "Gordie Howe is first to net 1,000 goals." *ESPN.com*

Wiles, Ed. The Rebel League: *The Short and Unruly Life of the World Hockey Association*. McClelland & Stewart, 2011

PHOTOS

"Milestone on ice: Howe's 1,000th goal" The Birmingham News. 8 Dec 1977. © 1977. The Birmingham News. All rights reserved. Reprinted with permission.

"Gordie Howe and his 1,000 goal puck." © 1977. The Birmingham News. All rights reserved. Reprinted with permission.

ALIEN ENCOUNTERS

THE SYLACAUGA METEORITE

Daley, Jason. "Piece of the Meteorite That Struck a Woman Sells for More Than Its Weight in Gold" *Smart News | Smithsonian Magazine*. 19 May 2017. https://www.smithsonianmag.com/smart-news/piece-meteor-hit-woman-sells-more-price-gold-180963262/

Eschner, Kat. "For the Only Person Ever Hit by a Meteorite, the Real Trouble

Began Later." *Smart News | Smithsonian Magazine.* 30 Nov 2016. https://www.smithsonianmag.com/smart-news/only-person-ever-hit-meteorite-real-trouble-began-later-180961238/

George, Alice. "In 1954, an Extraterrestrial Bruiser Shocked This Alabama Woman." *At the Smithsonian | Smithsonian Magazine.* 26 Nov 2019. https://www.smithsonianmag.com/smithsonian-institution/1954-extraterrestrial-bruiser-shocked-alabama-woman-180973646/

Hogan, R.E. (Buster). "AF takes meteor fragment to Ohio for closer look." *The Birmingham News.* 2 Dec 1954: Page 15

"How a Meteorite Ruined an Alabama Woman's Afternoon 65 Years Ago" By Chelsea Gohd 30 Nov 2019. https://www.space.com/meteorite-hit-alabama-woman-65-years-ago.html

Nobel, Justin. "The True Story of History's Only Known Meteorite Victim." *National Geographic News.* https://www.nationalgeographic.com/science/article/130220-russia-meteorite-ann-hodges-science-space-hit

Prondzinski, Mary Beth. "An American Meteorite In Paris." *Museum Chronicle Magazine, News from the University of Alabama Museums.* (Fall 2018)

PHOTOS

ABLE AND BAKER IN SPACE

"1959: Monkeys survive space mission." *BBC On This Day.* 29 May 1959. http://news.bbc.co.uk/onthisday/hi/dates/stories/may/28/

newsid_3725000/3725961.stm

"After 50 Years, Space Monkeys Not Forgotten" by Nell Greenfield Boyce
NPR, Morning Edition. https://www.npr.org/templates/story/story.
php?storyId=104578202

"Fancy quarters planned for Mrs. Space Monkey" *Spokane Chronicle*. 13 Aug
1959: Page 2

Forrester, Ellie May. "10 animals that have been to space." *Discover Wildlife*.
https://www.discoverwildlife.com/animal-facts/animals-in-space/

Gathany, Bob. "The incredible story of Miss Baker, the original space monkey."
AL.com. 27 May 2016. https://www.al.com/living/2016/05/miss_baker_-_
the_original_monk.html

"Memorial Set for Miss. Baker." *Times Daily*. 2 Dec 1984.

" Miss Baker." *Wikipedia.org*. https://en.wikipedia.org/wiki/Miss_Baker

PHOTOS

"Monkey Baker, payload of Jupiter (AM-18), poses on a model of the Jupiter
vehicle, May 29, 1959." Photo courtesy of NASA.

"Miss Baker, a squirrel monkey who made a historical flight aboard the Jupiter
(AM-18) in May 1959, is seen here in her viewing area where she resided at
the U.S. Space and Rocket Center." Photo courtesy of NASA.

"Jupiter (AM-18), suborbital primate flight with Able and Baker as its payload,
being ready for launch, May 28, 1959." Photo courtesy of NASA.

STARS FELL ON ALABAMA

"Carl Carmer." *Wikipedia.org*. https://en.wikipedia.org/wiki/Carl_Carmer

Greenshawn, Wayne. "Stars Fell on Alabama." *Encyclopedia of Alabama*.
http://www.encyclopediaofalabama.org/article/h-1596

Hall, John. "When Stars Fell on Alabama." *Alabama Heritage Magazine*. Winter 2000.

"Historic meteor storm inspired 'Stars Fell on Alabama' hit jazz song." *AL.com*.
10 Sept 2013. https://www.al.com/wire/2013/09/historic_meteor_storm_

inspired.html

"Leonids." *Wikipedia.org.* https://en.wikipedia.org/wiki/Leonids

"Meteors or Falling Stars." *Florence Gazette - The Democrat.* 21 Nov 1833.

Sanderson, Richard. "The night of raining fire. Leonid meteor storm". *Sky & Telescope. 1* Nov 1998. https://www.thefreelibrary.com/_/print/PrintArticle. aspx?id=21201970

Vulcan. "From Where I Stand" *The Birmingham News.* 21 Aug 1951.

ILLUSTRATION

Produced in 1889 for the Seventh-day Adventist book Bible Readings for the Home Circle. Adolph Vollmy in 1889. In the public domain

CLOSE ENCOUNTERS IN MOBILE

"Air Force Hunts For Saucers." *The Kansas City Times.* 17 Jun 1952: Page 7

Bouzereau, Laurent. "The Making of Close Encounters of the Third Kind." Published November 1977. Film. https://www.youtube.com/ watch?v=9e5CFErvYo0

"Close Encounters of the Third Kind." *Wikipedia.org.* https://en.wikipedia.org/ wiki/Close_Encounters_of_the_Third_Kind

Duncan, Andy. Alabama. *Curiosities: Quirky Characters, Roadside Oddities & Other Offbeat Stuff:* Globe Pequot Press, 2009.

Harvey, Alec. "'Close Encounters': Birmingham's Cary Guffey on Spielberg, the aliens and the movie that made him famous." *Alabama NewsCenter.* 6 Jul 2017.

Robinson, Jonathan E. *"Who are you people?"* Published 2017, Video.

PHOTOS

"Clapper board used during the filming of the movie "Close Encounters of the Third Kind" in Bay Minette, Alabama." Alabama Department of Archives and History. Donated by Alabama Media Group. Photo by Dave Hamby or

Martha Simmons, Mobile Press-Register.

"Richard Dreyfuss and other actors in Bay Minette, Alabama." Alabama
Department of Archives and History. Donated by Alabama Media Group.
Photo by Dave Hamby or Martha Simmons, Mobile Press-Register.

EXCEPTIONAL PEOPLE

WILLIAM RUFUS DEVANE KING - ALABAMA'S VICE-PRESIDENT

"Alabama Men's Hall of Fame." *Samford University*. https://www.samford.edu/
alabama-mens-hall-of-fame/inductees/King.html

"Alabama's William Rufus King, the 'Veep' who raced home to die." *The
Birmingham News*. 3 Aug 1952.

Brooks, Daniel Fate. "William Rufus King." *Encyclopedia of Alabama*.
http://www.encyclopediaofalabama.org/article/h-1886

"Obituary of William Rufus Devane King." *The Raleigh Register*. 23 Apr
1853: Page 3.

"Quiet Anniversary Ceremony Marks King Honors." *The Selma Time-Journal*. 24
March 1953.

Vice President William King, former Vice President of the United States."
Govtrack.us. https://www.govtrack.us/congress/members/william_
king/406377

"William Rufus King." *Wikipedia.org*. https://en.wikipedia.org/wiki/
William_R._King

"William R. King First Senator to Gain Vice Presidential Offer." *Senate.gov*.
https://www.senate.gov/about/officers-staff/vice-president/william-r-king-first-
senator-to-gain-vp-offer.htm

THE WICHAHPI COMMEMORATIVE STONE WALL - TOM'S WALL.

Allen, Sheronda. "A Wall Honors legacy of expelled Indian." *The Montgomery
Advertiser* . 18 Feb 2003.

Green, Bobbie. "Alabama wall tribute to ancestor." *The Daily Spectrum* (10 Oct 2014)

Halpern, Sylvia. "Tom Hendrix - The Stone Talker in Threets Alabama." 25 April 2011. Video. https://youtu.be/AVGuVnCUPgg

Kristoff, Anne. "Tom Hendrix is gone, but his wall lives on in Alabama" Alabama News Center. (12 April 2017) https://alabamanewscenter.com/2017/04/12/tom-hendrix-gone-wall-lives-alabama/

"Tom's Wall." *Visit Florence* https://www.visitflorenceal.com/directory/toms-wall/ 'Wichahpi Commemorative Stone Wall (Te-lah-nay's Wall) - Florence, Alabama."

NatchezTraceTravel.com. https://www.natcheztracetravel.com/natchez-trace-alabama/florence-tennessee-river/456-wichahpi-stone-wall.html

PHOTOS

Courtesy of Florence-Lauderdale Convention & Visitors Bureau. Visitshoals.com

FESS WHATLEY

"Erskine Hawkins." Wikipedia.org. https://en.wikipedia.org/wiki/Erskine_Hawkins

"John "Fess" Whatley Biography." Alabama Music Hall of Fame. 1991. https://www.alamhof.org/fess

Mathews, Burgin. "Magic City Jazz: John T. "Fess" Whatley and the roots of the Birmingham Jazz tradition." Thesis, UNC at Chapel Hill. 2020.

Mathews, Burgin. "Picturing Birmingham Jazz." Blog. 14 Jan 2019. https://burginmathews.com/2019/01/14/picturing-birmingham-jazz/

Price, William. "John T. "Fess" Whatley." Encyclopedia of Alabama. 23 Mar 2012. http://www.encyclopediaofalabama.org/article/h-3240

Sims, Jay. "The Fess Whatley Story." *The Huntsville Mirror*. 4 Feb 1956.

Zirpolo, Mike. "'Tuxedo Junction'Erskine Hawkins (1939) and Glenn Miller (1940)." Swing & Beyond. (22 Nov 2017): https://swingandbeyond.com/2017/11/22/tuxedo-junction-erskine-hawkins-1939-and-glenn-miller-1940/

PHOTOS

Students in print shop class with John T. "Fess" Whatley (toward the right) at Industrial High School. Birmingham Public Library, Department of Archives and Manuscripts. BBE137

Saxosociety Band. Courtesy of Patrick Cather. Image restoration by John Morse.

John T. "Fess" Whatley. Courtesy of Patrick Cather

RUTH ELDER - PILOT

Bair, Cinnamon. "Ruth Elder Just Wanted To Soar." *The Ledger.com*. 22 Apr 2007.

Barsanti, B. "Miss America of Aviation, Ruth Elder." *Flight Lines*. March 2020: Page 3.

Dunn, Hampton. "Ruth Elder: All-American Girl of the Jazz Age." *Sunland Tribune*. 1996: Vol. 22, Article 11.

"Ruth's Mother Sobs With Joy." *The Boston Globe*, 13 Oct 1927: Page 16

Holden, Henry M. *Ruth Elder*. Black Hawk Publishing. 1997, 2001.

"Katherine Stinson." *Wikipedia.org*. https://en.wikipedia.org/wiki/Katherine_Stinson

Lukes, Margaret M. "Is Woman's Place 'Up In The Air?'" *The Modesto Bee*. 20 Nov 1927: Page 24

"Nancy Batson Crews." Alabama Women's Hall of Fame. http://www.awhf.org/crews.html

"Ruth Elder." *Wikipedia.org*. https://en.wikipedia.org/wiki/Ruth_Elder

"Ruth Elder a Secretary Today" *Star-Gazette* (Elmira, New York). 26 Jun 1955: Page 36

PHOTOS

"Ruth Elder in front of plane." BIOE00333. San Diego Air and Space Museum Archive.

"Ruth Elder in cockpit of plane." BIOE00334. San Diego Air and Space Museum Archive.

"Ruth Elder's airplane was paid for by investors from Wheeling, West Virginia who saw great financial opportunity in the prospects for cashing in on the fame of a female Lindbergh. SI-90-5876. National Air and Space Museum, Smithsonian Institution."

LOU WOOSTER

"Baconsides." *Bhamwiki.com*. https://www.bhamwiki.com/w/Baconsides

Baggett, James. "Louise Wooster: Birmingham's Magdalen." *Alabama Heritage*. Fall 2005.

"Birmingham's Population." Birmingham Public Library. http://www.bplonline. org/resources/government/birminghampopulation.aspx

"Booth's Sweetheart Held Doomed to Disappointment." *The Salt Lake Tribune*. 28 Apr 1935: Page 32

Crider, Beverly. *Legends and Lore of Birmingham & Central Alabama*. History Press, 2014.

"Louise Wooster." *Bhamwiki.com*. https://www.bhamwiki.com/w/Louise_ Wooster

"Louise Wooster." Encyclopedia of Alabama. http://encyclopediaofalabama.org/ article/h-1862

"Louise Wooster is buried." *The Birmingham News*. 17 May 1913: Page 11

Peoples, Jared. "Birmingham Cholera Outbreak of 1873." Encyclopedia of Alabama. 16 June 2010: http://www.encyclopediaofalabama.org/ article/h-2607

"The Birmingham Cholera Epidemic of 1873" Libraries | UAB. https://library. uab.edu/locations/reynolds/collections/regional-history/cholera

"The Cholera" *The Troy Messenger*. 10 Jul 1873: Page 3

PHOTOS

"Lou Wooster Tombstone" photo by Shawn Wright

"Cyclists on 4th Avenue." Birmingham, Ala. Public Library Archives.

THE LAND

BIRMINGHAM'S CUT IN RED MOUNTAIN

Adams, Cathy Criss. *Worthy of Remembrance: A History of Redmont*. Redmont Park Historic District Foundation, 2002

"City gives loud 'No' to Red Mountain Study." *Birmingham News*. 19 Aug 1959: Page 1

"Iron Ore Seams Sign." *Bhamwiki.com*. http://www.bhamwiki.com/w/Iron_Ore_Seam_signs

Keith, Walling. "First a tunnel, then the moon." *The Birmingham News*. 20 Feb 1961: Page 20

Oramous, Phil. "Alabama Highway Projects Create Excitement in Variety of Fields." *The Selma Times-Journal*. 29 Dec 1970: Page 1

"Red Mountain Cut National Natural Landmark." *Encyclopedia of Alabama*. http://encyclopediaofalabama.org/article/m-9448

"Red Mountain Expressway." *Bhamwiki.com*. https://www.bhamwiki.com/w/Red_Mountain_Expressway

"Red Mountain Tunnel." *Bhamwiki.com*. https://www.bhamwiki.com/w/Red_Mountain_Tunnel

Spotswood, Francis. "Giant expressway, 280 job just routine in eyes of road engineer." *The Birmingham News*. 27 May 1963: Page 20

Whitley, Carla Jean. "Red Mountain: The past, present and future of Birmingham's foundation" *Birmingham Magazine*. https://www.al.com/bhammag/2015/01/red_mountain_the_foundation_of.html

PHOTOS

Historic American Engineering Record, Creator. Red Mountain Cut National Natural Landmark, U.S. 280 at Red Mountain, Birmingham, Jefferson County, AL. Jefferson County Alabama Birmingham, 1968. translateds by Benz, Suemitter Documentation Compiled After. Photograph. https://www.loc.gov/item/al1121/.

Construction Photos courtesy of Paul Ward, 1968.

WHERE DID THAT TOWN NAME COME FROM?

Duncan, Andy, *Alabama Curiosities: Quirky Characters, Roadside Oddities & Other Offbeat Stuff*, Globe Pequot Press, 2009. 288 pages

Encyclopedia of Alabama. http://encyclopediaofalabama.org/

Foscue, Virginia O. *Place Names in Alabama*, The University of Alabama Press, 1988. 184 pp.

Martin, Gay, *Alabama Off the Beaten Path*, 6th: A Guide to Unique Places. Globe Pequot; 2004

"What's in a Name? People, Habits give names to town." http://www.smuteye.com/name-smuteye.htm

PHOTOS

"Buzzard Roost Covered Bridge in Colbert County, Alabama, three miles west of Cherokee." Q3096. Alabama Department of Archives and History.

"Fruithurst and Pine Apple Signs" courtesy of Jimmy S. Emerson, DVM
Fruithurst - https://flic.kr/p/p8SnV and https://flic.kr/p/2hQo32Z
Pine Apple - https://flic.kr/p/98gkr

"Smut Eye Grocery" by Rivers Langley

KUDZU

Alabama Department of Archives & History Food for Thought Presentation

"The True Story of Kudzu, the Vine That Never Truly Ate the South by Bill Finch." 2018. https://www.youtube.com/watch?v=-39OEvVLT1U. Bill Finch is a writer and the principal conservation science advisor for the E.O. Wilson Biodiversity Foundation and a senior fellow for the Ocean Foundation.

Cope, Channing. *Front Porch Farmer*. Atlanta, Georgia: Turner E. Smith & Company, 1949.

https://babel.hathitrust.org/cgi/
pt?id=coo.31924003340340&view=1up&seq=1&skin=2021

Loewenstein, Nancy J., Stephen F. Enloe, John W. Everest, James H. Miller, Donald M. Ball, and Michael G. Patterson. *"History and Use of Kudzu in the Southeastern United States."* 8 Mar 2022. https://www.aces.edu/blog/topics/invasive-species/the-history-and-use-of-kudzu-in-the-southeastern-united-states/

Peters, Crocket. "The Miracle Vine. The story of kudzu." *TheAwl.com.* 29 August 2017.

https://www.theawl.com/2017/08/kudzu-the-miracle-vine/

PHOTOS

Kudzu photos by Shawn Wright

THE ARTISTS

SHE PAINTS ON SPIDER WEBS

"Closet of the Spiderweb Lady" https://www.roadsideamerica.com/story/35892

Cure, Sarah. "'Cobweb Painter' leaves behind fragile miniature masterpieces" *AL.com.* 7 Nov 2010. https://www.al.com/entertainment-times/2010/11/cobweb_painter_exhibit.html

"History of Cobweb Painting." Historical Collection, Huntsville Public Library. 1945

http://dreammakershop.com/annebradshawclopton/article3.html

Jones, Joyce L. "The Picture On The Web." *The Southerner Magazine.* May-June 1949.

McCualey, Pat. "Cobweb Painter Collects Art In Unusual Mediums."
Chattanooga Times. 24 August 1953.

McCormick, John. "Alabama Grandmother Paints Pictures On Cobwebs." *The
Atlanta Journal and Constitution Magazine.* 14 Sep 1952.

"Obituary Notice of Mrs. James Blount Clopton." *Huntsville Times.* 5 Feb 1956.
http://dreammakershop.com/annebradshawclopton/article6.html

Young, Lauren. "The Lost Art of Painting on Cobweb Canvases." *Atlas Obscura.*
6 Dec 2016. https://www.atlasobscura.com/articles/the-lost-art-of-painting-
on-cobweb-canvases

PHOTOS

"Anne Clopton viewing spider webs." Courtesy of HMCPL Special Collection.

"Anne Clopton's Big Spring at Huntsville." Courtesy of HMCPL Special Collection.

"Anne Clopton photographed in her studio" Courtesy of HMCPL Special
Collection.

THE PORTRAITS OF WILLIAM FRYE

Adams, E. Bryding, "William Frye, Artist," *Alabama Heritage 32.* Spring 1994: 30.

Adams, E. Bryding, "William Frye." 31 Jan 2012: http://www.
encyclopediaofalabama.org/article/h-3205

"Portrait Painting." *Alabama Beacon.* 21 Mar 1868: Page 3

Stanley, C.M. "More Portraits by Wm. Frye in Alabama." *The Montgomery
Advertiser* (26 Oct 1958): Page 11

"The Portraiture of William Frye." *Art of the American South.* https://southernart.
ua.edu/the-portraiture-of-william-frye/

"William Frye Obituary." *Huntsville Weekly Democrat.* 12 Jul 1872: Page 3

William (George Wilhelm Frey) Frye. Hunstville History Collection. http://
huntsvillehistorycollection.org/hh/index.php?title=Person:William_(George_
Wilhelm_Frey)_Frye

PHOTOS

Portraits of Ephraim Foster and Susan Foster in the collection of Leo Wright

"Big Spring at Huntsville" courtesy of HMCPL Special Collection

"Clement Comer Clay" courtesy of HMCPL Special Collection

CLARK BYERS SEES ROCK CITY

"American Icon Celebrates 60th Birthday" *The Call-Leader*. 21 Dec 1995: Page 3

Barn History. *SeeRockCity.com*. https://www.seerockcity.com/about/barn-history/

"Barn painter directed tourist to 'See Rock City'" *The Charlotte Observer*. 21 Feb 2004: Page 28

"Barn painter survived bulls, lightning" *The Daily News*. 17 Sep 1995: Page 14

"Caverns Hold Mystery Still." *The Montgomery Advertiser*. 14 Jun 1970: Page 58

Clark Byers, 89. *Chicago Tribune*. 22 Feb 2004: https://www.chicagotribune.com/news/ct-xpm-2004-02-22-0402220214-story.html

"Clark Byers, the Barnyard Rembrandt." *RelicRecord.com*. https://relicrecord.com/blog/clark-byers-barnyard-rembrandt/

Hollis, Tim. *See Alabama First*. The History Press, 2013

McMahan, Carroll. "Forty-Dollar Rembrandts." *Smoky Mountain Living*. 1 Feb 2018.

"Rock City signs dot nostalgic journeys" *The Daily News*. 17 Sep 1995: Page 14

"'See Rock City' Barns Vanishing" *AP*. (22 OCT 2014): https://www.tennessean.com/story/life/2014/10/22/see-rock-city-barns-vanishing-landscape/17715537/

"Seemingly endless beauty of Sequoyah Caverns" *The Anniston Star*. 24 May 1981: Page 50

Zoll, Rachell. "'See Rock City' Barn Painter Recalls Career." *Los Angeles Times*. 13 Sep 1998.

PHOTOS

Photos Courtesy of Rock City

Painted Barn - Highsmith, Carol M., 1946-, photographer. Carol M. Highsmith's America, Library of Congress, Prints and Photographs Division.

DOUGLAS LEIGH LIGHTS UP TIMES SQUARE

"Claridge Hotel in Times Square is Acquired by Douglas Leigh." *The New York Times*. 21 May 1964. p. 57.

"Birmingham Man Hits Big." *The Birmingham News* 8 Mar 1937. Page 7

Bloom, Ken *Broadway, An Encyclopedia*. Publisher Taylor & Francis. 2013. Ebook.

Cutler, Alan. *Smithsonian: Inside Smithsonian Research: A visual history of Times Square spectaculars.* https://web.archive.org/web/20100620172251/http://www.si.edu/opa/insideresearch/articles/V17_TimesSquare.html

"Douglas Leigh, The Man Who Lit Up Broadway, Dies at 92." *The New York Times*. 16 December 1999. Section B, Page 13.

Goldberg, Paul "Critics Notebook; A Snowflake weighs heavily on Fifth Avenue." *The New York Times*. 13 December 1984

Douglas Leigh - *Wikipedia*. https://en.wikipedia.org/wiki/Douglas_Leigh

Commissioners' Plan of 1811 - *Wikipedia*. https://en.wikipedia.org/wiki/Commissioners%27_Plan_of_1811

Gray, Christopher. "Streetscapes / Douglas Leigh, Sign Maker; The Man Behind Times Square's Smoke Rings." *New York Times*. 25 October 1998. Section 11, Page 5

Walker, Danton. "Broadway Cavalcade." *Daily News* (New York, New York) · 4 Oct 1940. Page 762

"Daytime Signs." *Daily News (New York, New York)*. 5 Aug 1942. Page 53

"One-Block Neon Sign is Due on Broadway." *Daily News* (New York, New York) · 26 Jun 1938. Page 70

"Tuesday in Birmingham." *The Birmingham News*. 30 Oct 1934, Tue · Page 18

"Birmingham Man Makes Big Hit On Great White Way." *The Birmingham News*. 8 Mar 1937. Page 7

"Lights o'Broadway His Brain Child." *Daily News*. 10 Jun 1945. Page 318

PHOTOS

Douglas Leigh maps Camel smoke-ring signs all over the country, between 1940 and 1945, from the Douglas Leigh Papers, 1903-1999 | Archives of American Art, Smithsonian Institution

Wonder Bread blimp, between 1945 and 1955, from the Douglas Leigh Papers, 1903-1999 | Archives of American Art, Smithsonian Institution

New York, New York. Camel cigarette advertisement at Times Square. By Vachon, John, 1914-1975, photographer. Farm Security Administration - Office of War Information photograph collection (Library of Congress). Library of Congress Control Number 2017846274.

Longacre Square South - Underhill, Irving -1960. Library of Congress Prints and Photographs Division

THE INVENTORS

MARY ANDERSON, INVENTOR OF THE WINDSHIELD WIPER

Bellis, Mary. "Biography of Mary Anderson, Inventor of the Windshield Wiper." *ThoughtCo*. 28 Jul 2019. https://www.thoughtco.com/mary-anderson-inventor-of-the-windshield-wiper-1992654

"Female Pioneers: Mary Anderson and Charlotte Bridgwood created windscreen wipers."

Denso.com. (8 May 2019). https://www.denso-am.eu/media/corporate-news/2019/deneur19_13_female-pioneers-mary-anderson-and-charlotte-bridgwood/

Letter to Mary Anderson from Dinning and Eckenstein - Photographs - Birmingham Public Library Digital Collections

"Mary Anderson, Windshield Wiper." *National Inventors Hall of Fame*. https://www.invent.org/inductees/mary-anderson

Olive III, J. Fred. "Mary Anderson." *Encyclopedia of Alabama.* http://www.
    encyclopediaofalabama.org/article/h-2553

Staff writer, "Windshield Wiper Inventor, Miss Mary Anderson, Dies."
    The Birmingham Post-Herald. 29 Jun 1953.

Stallworth, Clarke, "Southern belle invented wiper for windshield."
    The Birmingham News. 20 Feb 1977.

ANDREW JACKSON BEARD

"A Colored Inventor." *The Birmingham News.* 29 Sep 1898: Page 3

"A Negro's Success." *The Clayton Record.* 16 Oct 1903: Page 1

"An enterprising negro." *The Livingston Journal.* 5 Dec 1890: Page 6

"A southern negro's fortune." *Blade Enterprise.* 25 Dec 1890: Page 1

"Andrew Beard." *Bhamwiki.com.* https://www.bhamwiki.com/w/Andrew_Beard

Bron, Charles Allen. "Andrew Jackson Beard (1849-1921), an inventor."
    30 Aug 1969 https://bplonline.contentdm.oclc.org/digital/collection/
    p4017coll6/id/129/rec/97

Kindred, Ingrid. "Black Inventor Never Acclaimed" *Birmingham News.*
    13 Feb 1978.

Office of Public Affairs. "The Life of Andrew Beard - From Slave to Inventor."
    US Department of Transportation. https://www.transportation.gov/
    connections/life-andrew-beard-slave-inventor (broken link)

PHOTO

"Andrew Jackson Beard (1849-1921), an Inventor," Brown, Charles Allen.
    Inventions and Inventors-Birmingham. Birmingham, Ala. Public Library
    Archives.

JOHN PRATT - INVENTOR OF THE TYPEWRITER

"Business and Professional Woman seek to establish memorial to him" *The Coosa*

River News. 3 Nov 1922: Page 1

Crider. Beverly. "John Pratt of Centre was grandfather of the typewriter."
   AL.com, 14 Apr 2012.

Herkimer County Historical Society. *"The Story of the Typewriter 1873-1923."*
   26 Nov 2019.

"Inventor of the Typewriter Dies" *The Coosa River News.* 30 Jun 1905: Page 1

"John Pratt, early typewriter inventor from this area" *The Gadsden Messenger.*
   14 Sep 2012.

Mares, George Carl. *The History of the Typewriter.* Guilbert Pitman, London. 1909

Scientific American magazine, Vol. 17, Issue 1. New York, July 6, 1867

"Simple grave alone marks John Pratt's Fame" *The Anniston Star.* 30 Mar 1966:
   Page 7

"Sholes and Glidden typewriter." *Wikipedia.org.* https://en.wikipedia.org/wiki/
   Sholes_and_Glidden_typewriter

PHOTOS

John Pratt. Q8893. Alabama Department of Archives and History.

Typewriter invented by John Pratt in 1964. Q8894. Alabama Department of
   Archives and History.

Later model of the typewriter invented by John Pratt. Q8895. Alabama
   Department of Archives and History.

Acknowledgements

I want to thank my parents, Rhetta and Leo Wright for supporting me in everything I do. I have always loved the stories of their families that they shared with me and it inspired me to learn even more.

Thank you to my wife Leigh and sons, Aidan and Ethan. You might not know why I am doing all this, but you give me the space and support to do it. Love you guys!

Thanks to my brother Miles who helped me flesh out the final design for the cover.

The beauty of producing a podcast is you don't have to worry about photos. If they don't exist, no worries. If the expense is too high, no worries, you can still have a show. With this book, photos were important and I could not have done it without the generosity of people. I want to thank them here in no particular order:

Will Martin, Director of Marketing & Communications of the Florence-Lauderdale Convention & Visitors Bureau for the Tom's Wall photos.

Jimmy Emerson, DVM and Ginger Ann Brook who posted images on Flickr and let me use them for the town names story.

Meagan Jolley at Rock City for the Clark Byers and barn photos.

Caitlin Bowron, Archivist at Alabama Power Company for the WSY photos.

Patrick Cather for the Fess Whatley photos.

Jamie Sandford who happened to post a few of his father-in-laws photos of the cut in the mountain during construction. Thanks for being the go-between.

Paul Ward for letting me use the photos he took of the construction on the Red Mountain Cut from 1968.

Cait Monroe, Archivist, Special Collections Department, Downtown Huntsville-Madison County Public Library.

Meredith McDonough, Digital Assets Coordinator, Alabama Department of Archives and History.

Sydney Batten at Red Clay Media for help with Birmingham News images.

Catherine Champion, Assistant Archivist at the Birmingham Public Library.

Thank you to Jim Hahn, creator of Hahn's Historical Birmingham and Hahn's Historical Alabama pages on Facebook. I reached out early on to see if I could post about my Shades Cahaba podcast episodes and then Alabama Short Stories episodes to his readers. The community has been supportive and has helped me grow the podcast.

And thank you to everyone who took the time to listen to the podcast, to share it and send me positive feed back and words of encouragement.

About the Author

Shawn Wright is a graphic designer and creator of the Alabama Short Stories podcast. A lifetime citizen of Alabama, he lives in Homewood, Alabama, with his wife and two children. This is his second book. His first, *Shades Cahaba: The First 100 Years*, was published in 2020.

The author and his younger brother Miles, wishing you peace during Christmas 1970.

Podcasts

This book was created using the stories produced for the Alabama Short Stories podcast. You can listen to them at AlabamaShortStories.com. You can also find them where ever you listen to podcasts.

Shawn Wright's other podcast is the Shades Cahaba Oral History project. This limited edition podcast celebrated the 100th anniversary of this school in Homewood, Alabama. You can hear the episodes and read blog posts at ShadesCahabaHistory.com

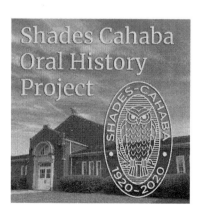